To Kate,

Merry Christmas as
you prepare for your
First Holy Communion.

Love,
Aunt Betty Conlon

Presented to . . .

_____

_____

by . . .

_____

date . . .

_____

"You are Peter, and on this rock I will build my Church, and the gates of the netherworld will not prevail against it."

—Matthew 16:18

# NEW CATHOLIC
# CHILDREN'S BIBLE

### INSPIRING BIBLE STORIES
### IN WORD AND PICTURE

By Rev. Thomas J. Donaghy

ILLUSTRATED IN FULL COLOR

CATHOLIC BOOK PUBLISHING CORP.
New Jersey

# Foreword

THROUGHOUT history the Bible has been divided into two major parts. The larger section depicts the creation of the world, the call of Abraham, the Mosaic Covenant, and God's loving relationship with the Jewish people. The shorter section deals for the most part with the Birth of Jesus, the Son of God, His life, His mission, His miracles, His Death on the Cross, and finally His Ascension into Heaven.

The Old Testament contains forty-six books, from the creation of the world to the time when Jesus Christ, the Son of God, would shortly be born, signaling the beginning of a new era. The New Testament contains twenty-seven books, from the time of the Birth of Jesus to His Death and Resurrection, as well as the writings of the Apostles, with emphasis on the sermons of Paul, Peter, and John.

Together these Testaments are of monumental importance in the history of God and the Church.

*Father Thomas J. Donaghy*

---

Nihil Obstat: Rev. James M. Cafone, M.A., S.T.D., Censor Librorum
Imprimatur: ✠ Most Rev. John J. Myers, J.C.D., D.D., Archbishop of Newark

The Nihil Obstat and Imprimatur are official declarations that a book or pamphlet is free of doctrinal or moral error. No implication is contained therein that those who have granted the Nihil Obstat and Imprimatur agree with the contents, opinions or statements expressed.

(T-645)

# Contents

# Introduction to the Old Testament

WHEN God created all of us, He wanted us to be with Him in a special way. Therefore, God, through the help of others, has given us a series of writings called the Bible. The Bible is divided into the Old Testament and the New Testament.

First we look at the Old Testament. It is as if we take a journey through thousands of years before the time of Jesus. We look in on the lives of God's people way back to the time of the first person God created. And it is important for us to know what God had in mind for us. So, He decided to inspire certain people to write down those truths He wanted them and us to know. He made sure everything written in the Old Testament would be without error. These truths show how much He loves all people. If people live the truths of the Old Testament, their salvation is assured.

Reading the events of the Old Testament will give us greater enthusiasm for reaching the goal of God's Kingdom. We will read of creation. We will come to know our first parents and their disobedience to God. The evil serpent will play a role in the fall of Adam and Eve. We will understand how dangerous the evil tempter can be for us.

Later, the great leader Moses comes on the scene. Through his efforts, a God-fearing society develops. We will learn the early ways His people gathered to praise the Lord. Also, the growing love of God's people for one another surfaces. And after the people of God have repented of their sins, we will follow them to the promised land.

We will discover the prophets. They wrote, preached and taught God's word, often at great peril. They were the chosen ones, who until the arrival of a Divine King would have great influence on God's people by their writings and preaching. The ongoing failures of human beings and the sins of preachers and kings led to the coming of a Divine King, Whom we call Jesus and Lord.

# GOD'S CREATION OF THE WORLD

*Genesis 1:1-31*

OUR catechism tell us that God is eternal. This means He always was and always will be. The catechism also says God is all love. For a long time, earth and the heavens as we know them did not exist. But our God wanted to give His love to others. He made the Angels, the highest form of creation, but not in His image and likeness. They were all spirit and nothing could restrain them.

Lucifer led all the Angels. When God told of His plans to create our world, Lucifer's pride caused him to say he would not cooperate. Angels loyal to Lucifer also refused to serve. Under the leadership of Archangel Michael, many Angels agreed to serve in any way God asked. Then a great battle took place between the good and bad Angels. Michael and his Angels drove Lucifer and his Angels into a place of eternal separation from God.

God's plans went ahead. The abyss of ocean waters that was darkness were brought under control by God's creating wind. We use the word "day" in telling of creation. But its meaning is different from our use of time. On the first day of creation, light was made, followed by the sky, which separated the waters. Birds appeared in the sky and fish and other kinds of animals in the oceans. Once the waters were separated, earth was created, where animals and human beings could live. From the earth's soil came plants and trees, giving humans vegetables and fruits.

With creation of sky and earth He controlled the waters. The sky, like an upside-down bowl, kept the waters in place. The wide open sky saw rain, snow and hail clouds form. These provided moisture for human, plant and animal life.

The sun provided favorable conditions for plants, animals and humans. The moon and stars gave direction and reduced light at night. Once creation was complete, on the sixth day, God created the first human being. God looked on His creation and was pleased. He contemplated the wonder of the human being, an image of Himself whom He would love as only a good God can.

# ADAM AND EVE

*Genesis 2:15—3:24*

GOD saved the best for last when He made human beings, because we are created in His image and likeness. What is even more exciting is that God made us in such a way that we are responsible for the earth.

Adam and Eve were the first humans. In the beginning, Adam was alone, placed by God in the Garden of Eden. The garden was somewhat like our large parks, filled with many beautiful trees. They provided shade from the sun. Though Eden was a wonderful place, God decided it was not good for Adam to be alone.

God put Adam into a deep sleep, and took one of his ribs. He built the rib into a woman, and brought the woman to Adam. Adam rejoiced at his companion, and the woman's name was Eve. Adam and Eve shared the same human substance. They were bonded by God's love and destined to live forever in the happiness and joy of Eden.

As time passed, a serpent, one of the cleverest of the animal world, came to Adam and Eve one day. He told them that God had a reason for telling them not to eat the fruit of a tree in the middle of Eden. Lying, he said if they ate the forbidden fruit they would not die. They would become like God and would know the difference between good and evil. So they ate the fruit. Suddenly, they realized they were naked and made clothes for themselves out of large leaves. At once, they knew good and evil, especially that all the good things of the Garden of Eden were no longer theirs. Moreover, they experienced a new sense of discomfort when they realized they had offended their loving God. It was the pangs of guilt they had never tasted, since they had never committed sin until that time.

God then cursed the serpent and condemned him to crawl on his belly, and it was separated from all the other animals. Eve was condemned to bear children in pain and would be subject to Adam. Adam was told by God that the earth would be cursed, and in order to grow fruits and vegetables he would have to work. "By the sweat of your brow you shall get bread to eat, until you return to the earth from which you were taken."

Adam and Eve were settled east of the Garden of Eden.

# CAIN AND ABEL

*Genesis 4:1—16*

AFTER Adam and Eve were put out of the Garden of Eden, Adam realized he had to work hard for their food. Meanwhile, Eve conceived a child, and after a painful delivery, her firstborn son Cain was born. Cain's name means "I have produced," which indicated what he was destined to do, and eventually he became a farmer.

Then Adam and Eve had a second child named Abel. While still young, Cain and Abel got along well. However, as Cain grew older he was known to be a mean person. Also Cain did not treat Abel very well. It may have been because Cain was a farmer, while Abel became a shepherd. When Abel tended his sheep, Cain would be at work in separate fields.

Eventually, Cain noticed that when he and Abel offered sacrifices to God, his offerings were not pleasing in God's eyes. Cain sacrificed the best of his fruits and vegetables, while Abel offered his best lambs. Cain saw that the smoke from Abel's offerings went straight up, but his blew off to the side. He felt this was a sign that God was not pleased with him and he became angry and jealous of Abel.

One day Cain said to Abel, "Let's go way out into the field." When they arrived at a spot far from their home, Cain attacked and killed Abel. Cain thought no one saw this. But God saw what Cain did to his brother. God asked Cain, "Where is your brother?" Cain, in a very disrespectful way asked God, "Am I my brother's keeper?" Still, God was not satisfied and asked Cain, "What have you done?" Then God proclaimed, "Your brother's blood cries out to me from the ground." Cain did not answer because he knew he was guilty of grave sin.

God banned Cain from working in the soil. He told Cain that if he tried to farm, the land would not produce. In telling Cain of his punishment, God reminded him, "You will stray restlessly upon the earth."

Cain pleaded with God, asking for some relief from his punishment. God was open to Cain's plea. He told Cain that He would place His mark on him. With this mark everyone would know that Cain, despite his grave sin, would be under God's protection. This prevented anyone from taking revenge on Cain because of his crime.

# GOD DECIDES TO PUNISH THE EARTH

*Genesis 6:5—7:24*

AS time passed, disobedience to God's ways began to grow. People became angry with each other. Even children began to fight and be mean to their brothers and sisters. Families would fight with other families.

All this disobedient conduct caused God to reconsider the people He created. As His feelings of regret began to develop, He asked Himself what He should do. He really did not want to punish the world, but He felt something had to be done. He thought of plague, but did not want to do that. Still, He realized He had to do something.

God knew there were some good people on earth. People like Noah and his extended families would be punished if God sent a plague or flood. That would be unjust. Also, He did not want to destroy the world's great beauty.

So, before punishing the world, God took the means necessary to preserve good people and save the world. He told Noah of a coming flood. He promised to save Noah's children and their families if they obeyed Him. They had to believe they would be safe in following Noah and had to help Noah with the work required to build a large boat or Ark. Not only were Noah and his relatives to be saved, but also Noah was to gather all different kinds of animals. Noah's neighbors saw the building of the Ark and asked Noah what was going on. He told them of the coming flood. Many made fun of Noah. Most people refused the last-minute invitation from God through Noah to renew their belief in God and save themselves.

The Ark was very high and very wide, having a number of decks. Food was gathered. When the Ark was complete, word went out to all who were planning to go to come to the Ark. The animals were marched on board. Noah made one last appeal to local folks, but they refused to join him. Soon after everyone was on board, the weather changed noticeably. The skies grew darker and darker with heavy rain clouds. Then a massive downpour began. The local people continued to watch with disbelief, feeling they were in for a day or two of rain. But the steady rain remained for one hundred fifty days, and the mountains eventually disappeared under the mounting waters.

# THE FLOOD

*Genesis 7:10—8:20*

FROM ancient times water has always had special meaning. The early Hebrews looked upon water as a font of both life and destruction. When God decided to send the flood in Noah's time, He allowed the waters to be released. "All the fountains of the great deep burst apart, and the floodgates of the sky broke open."

In Noah's time, when the water began to rise, people and animals moved toward the high ground for safety. After a few weeks, the water became so deep that it lifted the Ark from its giant construction cradle. The Ark, waterproofed throughout, floated on the water's surface.

Meanwhile, people and animals not on the Ark fought among themselves for places on the highest hills and mountains. Things went from bad to worse, and the water continued to rise until it was twenty-five feet higher than the tallest mountain. By that time, "all that swarmed the earth were drowned." And all people outside the Ark perished.

Eventually God took the necessary steps to bring the flood to an end. He created a great wind that swept over the earth. As a result, the waters began to go down. After one hundred fifty days without rain, the waters were so low that on the seventh day of the seventh month, the Ark came to rest on the mountains of Ararat. For another three months, the waters continued to go down. Finally, on the first day of the tenth month, the tops of the mountains appeared.

Then Noah opened a window on the Ark and sent out a bird so see what would happen. The bird soon returned since there was still no place to land. Later a second bird was sent, and it too returned. Finally, Noah sent a third bird. It was gone a long time and did not return. Noah took this as a sign that it would soon be safe to leave the Ark.

While there was some impatience among the people, Noah wanted to be sure there would be dry land outside the Ark when they left it. As they finally left the Ark, they stepped onto dry land. All gathered under Noah's leadership, and a great ceremony of praise took place. They were thankful to God for their safety, and, at the same time, they realized the benefits of their obedience to the Lord.

# A COVENANT WITH NOAH

*Genesis 9:1-17*

THE great flood lasted about one year and ten days. Although Noah knew the flood waters were going down when the Ark settled on Mount Ararat, God told Noah when to leave the Ark. As soon as the people left the Ark, Noah gathered them together and he offered a sacrifice of thanksgiving to God. They appreciated the fact that God had preserved so many animals for their use. After such a long time under water, the earth and all its survivors needed much help.

God understood the challenging conditions Noah's family faced. So, He decided to make sure there would be enough people to do the necessary work for society to survive in the future. God told Noah's people how pleased He would be if they would multiply. All families would need many new members. God had given the same kind of advice to Adam and Eve in the Garden of Eden. The punishment of the flood had come about through the disobedience of the descendants of Adam and Eve.

At the same time, the Lord did not want His people to live in fear of another flood. So He made a promise that for all time the world would never again be destroyed by flood. In ancient times, these kinds of promises were called covenants.

While it is true God's word and promise were sufficient guarantee, still the Lord gave His people a sign for all time that the earth would never be destroyed by water, the rainbow. It is always a reminder of God's promise, His love and forgiveness. God not only forgave Noah and his descendants, but also continues to forgive all peoples today.

While speaking with Noah about His covenant, God made other statements that explain some features of humanity. He told Noah his people could kill animals for food. However, God did not want people to eat the blood of animals, since blood is a sign of life. God reserved to Himself the right to control life. Human life was never to be destroyed by another human. Since people are created in the image and likeness of God, only He determines the length of anyone's life.

With God's covenant complete, Noah's people began settling the world. Some moved far from the Mount Ararat region. Noah's influence began to weaken, and disobedience and rebelliousness grew.

# THE TOWER OF BABEL

*Genesis 11:1-9*

OVER time, as people spread through the lands, groups began to form into communities. Trade developed and encouraged people to go from place to place. At the same time, civil laws were established. Further, rivalries grew among the settlements. Soon people turned to strong leaders for protection.

Since people spoke the same language, it was easy to settle in different places. As Babylon grew larger and larger, the people decided to build a large tower of brick. Tall watchtowers were common at that time, and they were used for lookouts.

God was concerned over the tower at Babylon. The people seemed to be building the tower for two separate reasons. Some said, "Come, let us build ourselves a city and tower, whose top may reach to heaven and so make us a name, lest we be scattered all over the earth." It was not unusual for a city to want to be well known. People hoped their city's name would spread, and visitors from other places would want to view their unique tower. This would have been perfectly normal. However, some who wanted to build into the sky were attempting to overcome the Lord's control

over the earth. In addition, the tower was becoming a source of pride for its builders as well as offensive in God's eyes.

When the Lord implied that Noah and his descendants should multiply and fill the earth, He meant adding numbers through childbirth. He also wanted His people to move throughout the then-known world. The tower builders did not want their people to scatter, thinking it would weaken their kingdom.

Since God had concerns about the tower at Babylon, He "came down" to earth to see what the people were doing and said, "If now, while one people, all speaking the same language, they have begun to do this, nothing will ever stop them from doing whatever they propose to do. Let us go down there and confuse their language, so that no one will understand what the other says."

The work on the tower then came to a halt. Workers could no longer understand each other. Moreover, as the result of the many new languages, it became very difficult for communities to remain united. Then out of Babylon a great migration took place. At the same time, trade and travel became more of a challenge.

# GOD CALLS ABRAHAM AND SARAH

*Genesis 12:1    17:27*

WITH people living across the then-known world, the story of God's people shifts to individuals like Abram, later Abraham, and Sarai or Sarah. God chose Abram for a leadership role among His people. The promise or blessing for Abram would be a source of great happiness for him and his descendants. In Abram's favorable response to God, he would be blessed. At the same time, all the communities of Abram's era would see Abram as favored by God.

The Bible tells us, "Abram departed as the Lord directed." There seems to be no doubt that Abram's deep faith and generous response to God won him God's favor.

Abram left the city of Ur and went with his family to another land. His wife Sarah, his nephew Lot and all his families, with their belongings, followed Abram. They stopped first at Shechem and saw that the land was overcome with famine at that time. So Abram's group went to Egypt to obtain the food necessary to survive. Although Abram feared Egypt's Pharaoh, God watched over him

and his followers. They were soon able to leave Egypt unharmed.

God continued to bless Abram and Lot to such a degree that they both became very wealthy. Then they decided to go separate ways. Abram gave Lot first choice as to where to settle. Lot chose the southern lands, which happened to be the best. Abram's unselfishness pleased God, and He promised Abram descendants as numerous as the stars in the sky.

For his part, Abram promised always to walk in God's presence, and to live a blameless life. Also, God gave Abram a new name, "Abraham," which means "father of many nations." To seal the agreement with God, Abraham made a sacrifice. God was pleased and promised that Abraham's son and grandson would inherit Abraham's lands.

Still, Sarah did not have any children. She sent her female servant, Hagar, into Abraham's tent. Hagar had a son, but God told Abraham that Hagar's son would not share God's covenant with Abraham. God promised Abraham and Sarah a son whose name would be Isaac. Abraham and Sarah trusted God completely and waited for God's promise.

# GOD VISITS ABRAHAM AND SARAH

*Genesis 18:1—19:29*

ABRAHAM and Sarah's faith was really put to the test concerning the birth of a child to them. They were already past ninety years of age, but they continued to wait in hope. One very warm day, Abraham was seated outside their tent seeking a cool spot. Eventually, three strangers were walking along the pathway. As was the custom of that time, Abraham stood and invited the strangers to have something to eat. Once they were seated in the shade of their tent, Abraham asked Sarah to bake some bread. Meanwhile, Abraham gave them some milk to drink, and then he prepared a calf for the evening meal.

Abraham did not realize that the three strangers were God and two of His Angels. Abraham's generosity pleased God. He asked Abraham where Sarah was, and he said Sarah was in the tent. Then God told Abraham that Sarah would give birth to a son within the year. Sarah, who was listening, burst out laughing when she heard of her future son, because they were so old.

God heard Sarah laugh and was concerned that Abraham and Sarah did not trust more fully in Him. The Lord said to Abraham, "Why did Sarah laugh and say, 'Am I really to bear a child in my old age?' Is anything too wonderful for the Lord to do?" God promised to return and then Sarah would have a son. The child would be called Isaac, which means "laughter."

God continued to trust Abraham and told him of His plans to destroy the cities of Sodom and Gomorrah, where Lot, Abraham's nephew, and his family lived. Abraham was upset when he thought of the innocent people living there. So, he asked God if fifty good people could be found living there, would the cities be spared. God told Abraham if fifty good people could be found, the cities would not be destroyed.

Then Abraham, humble and respectful, continued to press the Lord. Each time Abraham lowered the number of good people, God would agree. Soon they reached the number ten. But ten good people could not be found. The cities were destroyed, while Lot and his family were saved. God was very willing to save the innocent few.

# ISAAC MARRIES REBEKAH

*Genesis 24:1-67*

GOD'S promise of a child to Abraham and Sarah came true, despite their age. Isaac's birth brought great joy to Abraham, Sarah, their relatives and friends. He was circumcised according to God's wishes and grew up to be a strong young man.

Abraham's faith was tested when God asked him to sacrifice Isaac. Up to the very moment when Abraham was about to strike Isaac, Abraham's faith never wavered! God called to Abraham to stop him, and, at the same time, praised Abraham for his faith and obedience. God then told Abraham his descendants would be as numerous as the stars of the sky and the sands of the seashore.

A short time later, Sarah, just over 120 years old, died. Abraham was very sad and wept a long time. Through the goodness of the people of Hebron, he was able to buy a cave in which to bury Sarah. Abraham, too, was getting very old, and he was concerned that Isaac have a good wife. Abraham gave his top servant the task of searching for a young woman to marry Isaac, though she was not to be a Canaanite.

The servant took ten of Abraham's camels loaded with all kinds of gifts. He went to the city of Nahor where he rested the camels near the town well. He would ask for a drink, hoping the woman who gave him one would also water his camels. Rebekah, the grandniece of Abraham, came by, and unknowingly fulfilled the servant's plan. Immediately showered with gifts, Rebekah invited the servant to her mother's home. He spoke with her family, asking permission to take Rebekah with him to marry Isaac.

Rebekah agreed to go, and the fertility blessing was given her. When they arrived at Abraham's lands, Isaac was out working the fields and saw the caravan return. Rebekah saw Isaac from a distance and veiled her face, since the groom was not to see the bride until the wedding ceremony. Afterward, Rebekah and Isaac fell in love and were blessed by God. In his newfound love for Rebekah, Isaac found great comfort and overcame the sorrow surrounding Sarah's death. Abraham married again and had many children. At his death at age 175, Abraham had deeded all he owned to Isaac.

# ESAU AND JACOB

*Genesis 25:19-34*

FOR a long time following their wedding, Isaac and Rebekah did not have any children. This was a great disappointment for them. Isaac pleaded with God for children, and his prayer was answered. Rebekah became pregnant. After some time, Rebekah became aware she was to have twins. But her joy and anticipation were soon turned to disappointment. Rebekah could feel and was surely certain that the two unborn children in her womb were struggling with one another. Rebekah asked God what this great inner struggle could mean. The Lord informed Rebekah that her two children were to be leaders of two separate nations. Those two nations would eventually war with one another.

Once the twins were born, they were given the names Esau and Jacob. Esau was "reddish" in skin tone and "hairy." Also, he was a hunter and later had a reputation of being wild and rough. The second twin, Jacob, was favored by his mother Rebekah, because he seemed more gentle. Jacob later became a shepherd and seemed more peaceful than Esau. At the same time, it was clear to other family members and neighbors that Esau was favored by his father Isaac. A natural competition grew between Esau and Jacob. As the twins grew older, their differences became a significant part of the direction Isaac's descendants would take.

Esau seemed to be interested in having his way in family matters. With his tendency to make quick decisions, he became an easy target for his brother Jacob. Jacob also wanted to have more control in the family. Since Esau was the firstborn, by law, he inherited the family birthright. According to law, that meant Esau would receive a double portion of the family inheritance. This was a disappointing circumstance for even the mild-mannered Jacob. Since Jacob was aware of Esau's hastiness, one day when Esau came from hunting, he told Jacob he was starving. He wanted some of Jacob's lentil soup, which Esau called "red stuff." Jacob told Esau he could have some if Esau would give Jacob his birthright. Esau, who thought he would not live long, answered, "Look, I'm nearly dying of starvation. What good will my birthright do me?" Jacob realized his plan was working and replied, "Swear to me," and Esau agreed.

Then Jacob gave Esau some bread and lentil stew. Esau ate and left. Many believed Esau had little interest in his birthright. Still, family matters were far from settled. Isaac, who was becoming more and more feeble, still preferred his firstborn son Esau over Jacob. Later on, Jacob would try to take Esau's place with trickery.

# ISAAC AND JACOB

*Genesis 27:1-29*

ONE day when Isaac was quite elderly and nearly blind, he called Esau into his tent and told him, "As you can see, I am old and do not know how soon I may die." He asked Esau to take his quiver and bow and go out into the country to hunt for some game. When he was satisfied with his hunting, Esau was to prepare an appetizing meal for his father. "Bring it to me to eat so that I may give you my special blessing." In the ancient world, deathbed blessings were considered to be very special and were eagerly sought. Esau obeyed his father.

However, Rebekah had listened to the conversation between Isaac and Esau. So, when Esau had gone to the country to hunt, Rebekah called Jacob and told him the story. Rebekah really wanted Jacob to get Isaac's special blessing. So, Rebekah told Jacob to go to his flocks and select two choice lambs and bring them to her. Rebekah would then prepare a tasty dish she already knew Isaac liked best. Rebekah wanted Jacob to take the meal to Isaac in order to receive the special blessing.

Jacob feared that Isaac might discover the plan between him and Rebekah, because Esau was very hairy, while Jacob was fair. And Jacob did not want to be caught in a lie for fear he would be cursed. Rebekah told Jacob that if their plan was discovered, his mother would take the curse upon herself. The lambs were made into Isaac's favorite dish. Rebekah gave Jacob Esau's finest clothes. She then took the skin of the lambs and covered Jacob's arms and hairless neck. Then Jacob went to Isaac with the cooked lamb and bread that Rebekah had made.

Jacob went to his father and called to him. Isaac replied, "Which son are you?" Jacob replied, "I am Esau, your first-born." Jacob then asked Isaac to sit forward "and take then of my game, so that you may grant me your special blessing." Isaac asked Jacob to come closer so he could touch him to determine if he really was Esau. He felt Jacob's false hairy arms and neck, but still believed the voice was Jacob's. Isaac said, "Are you truly my son Esau?" Jacob said yes. Isaac ate the meal and gave Jacob his blessing. Jacob left his father quickly, since he was warned by Rebekah that Esau was about to arrive.

# JACOB AND ESAU MEET AGAIN

*Genesis 27:30-45; 33:1-20*

WHEN Esau returned to Isaac's tent, he offered his father some of the game he had hunted and prepared. Then he asked Isaac for his special blessing. Isaac said, "Who are you?" Esau answered, "Your firstborn son." Isaac then realized what had happened with Jacob and he began trembling severely. He told Esau what Jacob had done and how the blessing was given to Jacob and could not be taken back. Esau pleaded, "Have you reserved no blessing for me?" Isaac then told Esau how he had already appointed Jacob as Esau's master, "and I have given to him all his kinsmen as servants. I have enriched him with grain and wine. What is there for you?"

Esau was very angry and left Isaac. He planned to get even with Jacob. He decided that Jacob would come to Isaac's funeral in the future. Esau would then kill Jacob. Rebekah, meanwhile, learned of Esau's violent plan. She warned Jacob to go away. Jacob then went to find his uncle Laban and stayed with him until Esau's anger passed.

Laban received Jacob with great kindness and introduced him to his two daughters, Leah and Rachel. Jacob found Rachel more to his liking and asked Laban for Rachel's hand in marriage, even though she was younger. In return, Jacob agreed to work seven years for Laban. Laban tricked Jacob into completing his marriage responsibilities with Leah. When Jacob discovered this, Laban agreed to give Jacob Rachel as well as Leah. Then, Jacob was required to do an additional seven years work for Laban.

As many years passed, Jacob had a number of children. In later life Rachel gave birth to a son who was named Joseph. After this, Jacob was anxious to leave Laban's lands and go near to his homelands. Jacob, before leaving, tricked Laban into giving him a major portion of his lands and possessions. Unaware of what Jacob did, Laban gave his blessing and Jacob, with his family, left Laban's dwellings.

On the way, Jacob saw Esau approach with four hundred men. Fearful, Jacob divided his children between Leah and Rachel and moved them aside. Staff in hand, Jacob bowed seven times toward Esau. His humble gestures moved Esau. Esau ran to Jacob and hugged him, while kissing his neck and weeping. Esau asked about the children, and Jacob said they were God's gifts. Esau seemed joyful over Jacob's return. And Jacob felt their meeting was like an experience with God. However, there seemed to be a hidden lack of trust between the brothers. Esau was persuaded to go on without Jacob, while Jacob traveled to Shechem.

# JOSEPH AND HIS BROTHERS

*Genesis 37:1-36*

JACOB, having settled in the land of Canaan, where his father had lived for some time, gave much attention to his children and their families. However, his favorite son was Joseph, born of Rachel, and second youngest of the brothers. Jacob loved the fact that Joseph was Rachel's child. And Jacob made no secret of his favoritism.

As in many families, there were jealousies which developed, especially among Joseph's older brothers. At the same time, there were good reasons for the brothers' hostile feelings toward Joseph. The first centered around a long tunic or coat which Joseph's father gave him. It was a special coat due to its length and the wide sleeves. A Greek writing called it a "coat of many colors." And that has become a popular idea in our time. A second issue among the brothers was Joseph's tendency to speak of his many dreams, for which they called him "the dreamer." So, Joseph was not popular among his brothers when he told them of a dream where he would be ruler over them.

Once while Joseph's brothers were tending their father's flocks a great distance from the house, Jacob sent Joseph out to check on them. The brothers saw him coming and made plans to punish him. They were so angry and jealous over Joseph that some wanted to kill him. But Reuben persuaded the group not to kill him but to put him into a dry well. When Ishmaelite merchants approached, they decided to sell Joseph to them. With Joseph out of the way, the brothers smeared blood on Joseph's coat and took it back to Jacob to convince him that Joseph had been killed by a wild animal.

When the merchants arrived in Egypt, they sold Joseph into slavery. He was purchased by Potiphar, but after some time, Potiphar's wife accused Joseph of doing evil things, and Joseph was placed in an Egyptian prison. Joseph continued to share his interest in and evaluation of his dreams with other prisoners. This would prove to be a turning point in his life later on.

When Joseph's brothers arrived back home with the tragic news of Joseph's "death," using the very blood-stained coat as evidence which had earlier caused so much hostility, Jacob was inconsolable. He tore his clothes, put on sackcloth, and went into mourning over a long period of time.

# JOSEPH EXPLAINS
# THE DREAM OF PHARAOH

*Genesis 40:1—41:57*

FOR two years Joseph had remained in a dungeon. Pharaoh's cup-bearer had been in prison with Joseph. He was the official keeper and taster of Pharaoh's wines. He remembered that while in jail, Joseph told his fellow inmates that dream interpretation belongs to God. He spoke to Pharaoh about Joseph at a time when Pharaoh was in distress over dreams. Pharaoh sent for Joseph and explained to him that all the sages and magicians of Egypt had failed to interpret dreams.

When Pharaoh asked Joseph if he could interpret dreams, Joseph answered, "It is not I, but God who will give Pharaoh a favorable answer." Pharaoh told Joseph that in his dreams, he was standing along the Nile River. He saw seven fat cows grazing along the riverbank. Then seven thin cows came and ate the seven healthy cows. Still, the cows looked just as sickly.

In another dream, Pharaoh saw seven sickly ears of grain consume seven healthy ears without improving their appearance. Joseph told Pharaoh God was telling him of the future. Egypt was about to experience seven years of abundant harvest, followed by seven years of terrible famine. Since Pharaoh had the dreams twice, the coming events were confirmed by God and would soon begin. Joseph suggested that Pharaoh put someone in charge of all lands so that they would be regulated so as to yield the most abundant grain possible. This grain should be stored in every town in anticipation of the famine.

Pharaoh appointed Joseph in charge of all Egyptian lands. Pharaoh gave him a signet ring as a royal seal. Joseph received a gold chain, linen robes, chariots and criers to clear the way for him, all indications of Joseph's new noble standing.

During years of plenty, Joseph's actions prepared Egypt for the famine. Pharaoh was pleased with Joseph's saving activities. He gave Joseph in marriage to Asenath. With Asenath, he had two sons.

Joseph was indeed fruitful. When famine came and people cried to Pharaoh for food, he sent them to Joseph. All cities that stored grain were opened. And the rest of the world looked to Egypt for grain.

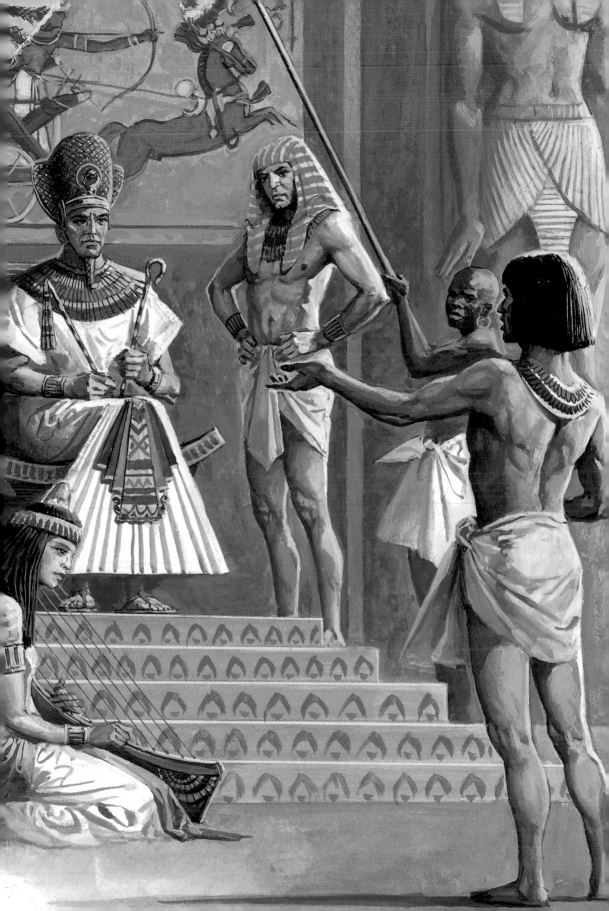

# BABY MOSES

*Exodus 2:1-10*

THE great famine continued to bring much suffering to the unprepared Israelites. Eventually, Joseph and all his brothers and their generation died. Still, the Israelite people continued to experience great numerical growth in Egypt.

Later, a new Egyptian Pharaoh ascended the throne. He knew nothing of Joseph. The new king was concerned over the rapid growth in numbers among the Israelites. He feared the Israelites would soon outnumber the Egyptians. He also believed the Israelites might join Egypt's future enemies in wartime. He ordered his supervisors to put the Israelites into forced labor, but the more they were forced to labor, the quicker their numbers increased. Then he told Hebrew midwives that if Hebrew women gave birth to boys they should be killed, but they did not do exactly as they were told. Angered, Pharaoh proclaimed to all his people, "Throw into the river every male child that is born of the Hebrews, but every daughter may live."

Later a man of the family of Levi and a Levite woman were married. They had a son. The mother kept the child for three months, but realized she could no longer hide him. Making a basket of papyrus, she put her child in the basket and placed it in the reeds along the river. His older sister, hiding herself, watched out for the basket.

When Pharaoh's daughter came to the river to bathe, she saw the basket and called to one of her maids to bring the basket to her. When she opened the basket, she saw the crying baby. Moved with pity, she said to her maid, "It is a little Hebrew boy." Then the baby's sister, who had been watching, spoke up and asked if she should get a Hebrew woman to nurse the child. When Pharaoh's daughter agreed, the child's own mother was called.

Pharaoh's daughter said, "Take care of this child, and I will pay you well." Joyfully the woman took the child and nursed it. Pharaoh did nothing about the Hebrew child since his daughter was attached to the boy. In three years, the woman brought her son to Pharaoh's daughter and was paid for her services. Pharaoh's daughter adopted the boy according to Egyptian law and she called him Moses, which means "is born."

# MOSES AT THE WELL

*Exodus 2:11-22*

AS Moses began to grow into a young man, he began to understand his relationship to his foster mother and his birth mother. He became more and more interested in the Israelites who really were his people. Growing fond of the Israelites, he left his foster mother's place to visit with relatives and friends.

One time, when Moses was fully grown, he visited his relatives. He began to resent their having to live in forced labor. Moses saw an Egyptian hit one of his relatives. Thinking he was alone, and seeing no other Egyptians, he killed the Egyptian who attacked his relative. He then buried the man in the sand. The next day, he saw two Israelites fighting. Moses asked, "Why are you striking your brother?" One replied, "Do you intend to kill me as you killed the Egyptian?" This reaction frightened Moses, since he realized his secret must be known.

Pharaoh also heard of the matter and planned to have Moses killed. Moses fled to the Midian lands. As he was seated near a well in Midian one day, people were coming to the well to get water for their animals. Then seven young ladies who were the daughters of a Midian priest stopped to get water for their father's flock. Some shepherds came and chased the young women. Moses became angry and stood up to defend the women. He then watered their flock for them. They thanked Moses and returned home.

Their father Reuel (also known as Jethro) noticed they had returned home early, and said, "How have you returned so quickly today?" The daughters, calling Moses an Egyptian, explained how he had chased the shepherds and quickly watered their flock. Reuel asked where the man was and wanted to know why the women left Moses at the well.

They returned with Reuel's invitation to come and dine with them. After the meal, Moses agreed to live with them. Reuel gave Moses his daughter Zipporah in marriage. Their first child was called Gershom, for Moses said, "I have become an exile in a foreign land." Respected widely in the tribe of Reuel, it was from there that Moses' reputation as a man of God and a future leader of His people began to grow. God in His own ways soon brought Moses into contact with Him to share His plans for Moses and the Israelites.

# THE BURNING BUSH

*Exodus 3:1-22*

WHEN Moses settled into life with his wife and children, his father-in-law Jethro hired him. Conditions had not changed for the Israelites who were enslaved in Egypt. They cried out to God because of the bitter burdens of slavery. God heard their cry, aware of His covenant with Abraham, Isaac and Jacob. God then decided to remedy the conditions the Israelites suffered.

While Moses was tending Jethro's flock of sheep, he was leading them through the desert toward God's mountain, Mount Horeb. Moses was astonished to see an Angel of the Lord who appeared to him in a bush of flaming fire. Moses was so taken with the burning bush that he looked at it for a time. Then he realized that even though the bush was on fire, it was not being consumed. So, Moses decided to go nearer the bush to see why it did not burn up.

When God saw Moses approach the bush, He spoke: "Moses, Moses!" Then God said, "Draw no closer! Cast aside the sandals from your feet, for the place where you are is holy." God's presence in the bush cast the fear of instant death over Moses. It was believed that no one could see God and live. So, Moses covered his face so as not to look on God.

When Moses calmed himself, God told him He had heard the Israelites' pleadings. God spoke of the afflictions of His people under the cruel scourge of slavery in Egypt. He further told Moses He had come "down" to rescue His people. Then God shared His plans with Moses to lead the Israelites out of Egypt and send them into abundant lands "filled with milk and honey."

God told Moses he would send him to Pharaoh to lead the Israelites out of Egypt. Moses protested as to why he should go to Pharaoh as the Israelite leader. But God promised to be with Moses, and as a sign all would go well, He said the Israelites would come with Moses to Mount Horeb to praise and thank God for their release.

If Pharaoh were to ask Moses what the God's name was Who sent him, Moses was to answer, "I AM." Moses was to gather the Israelite elders and tell them God heard their cry and would rescue them. God said Pharaoh would resist, but the powerful hand of God would force the Egyptians to beg the Israelites to leave.

# MOSES BEFORE PHARAOH

*Exodus 6:10—7:24*

AS Moses thought over the challenge before him, he heard the Lord speak. God told Moses to repeat to Pharaoh all that God had told Moses concerning the release of the Israelites from Egypt. Moses answered that he was a poor speaker and did not think Pharaoh would listen to him. God answered, "See, I have made you as a god to Pharaoh, and your brother Aaron shall serve as your prophet." God told Moses again to tell Pharaoh all God had told him before, and said, "Your brother Aaron shall tell Pharaoh to let the Israelites go from his land."

Moses and Aaron were assured by God that although Pharaoh would be stubborn and refuse their request, God would bring "great pumishment" on Pharaoh and his people in order to convince Pharaoh to let God's people leave. Although God would punish Pharaoh and his people if he refused God's request, the Israelites in Egypt would not be harmed.

So, Moses and Aaron did as they wore told. Moses was eighty years old and Aaron eighty-three when they appeared before Pharaoh. God told Moses and Aaron if Pharaoh wanted a sign, they were to throw their staffs to the floor before Pharaoh, and these would be changed into serpents. When Pharaoh asked for a sign, Moses dropped his staff and it became a snake. Pharaoh asked his wisemen to do the same, and their staffs became serpents. But Aaron's staff, now a serpent, swallowed all the other snakes.

Pharaoh would not give in. Moses and Aaron were amazed at his refusal. God calmed their surprise by telling them of disasters in store for Egypt. God told Moses to go to the riverbank and tell Pharaoh the Hebrew God had sent him to ask for His people's release. Since he refused, a sign would be given showing Moses' God was Lord of all.

In view of Pharaoh Moses proclaimed, "I will strike the river water . . . until it turns into blood." Moses warned further that pollution would be so bad that in all Egypt people would be unable to drink water. At the Lord's command, Aaron raised his staff over the river and all water sources throughout the land turned into blood. However, the Egyptian magicians at Pharaoh's command did the same thing. The waters were clear again, and Pharaoh stood firm in his refusal.

# THE PLAGUES: LOCUSTS

*Exodus 10:1-20*

SINCE Pharaoh remained firm in his refusal to let the Israelites go, God continued to send plagues. A plague of frogs covered Egypt and its people. This was followed by gnats, which swarmed over a large area. Still, Pharaoh would not give in. Then the Lord sent swarms of flies over Egypt, except where the Israelites lived. Later a disease afflicted all the Egyptian horses, asses, camels, herds, and flocks without touching the Israelites' animals. Pharaoh still refused, and God unleashed fierce hail on Egypt.

Due to Pharaoh's hardness of heart, God planned an eighth plague. The Lord was becoming very upset with Pharaoh and sent Moses and Aaron to speak with Pharaoh for a third time. At the same time, it became clear Pharaoh's servants were becoming alarmed with Pharaoh and his continued refusals. Meanwhile, the Egyptian people were going through terrible sufferings from the plagues. During their third appearance before Pharaoh, Moses and Aaron asked that the entire Israelite community be permitted to go into the desert to worship their God.

Since Pharaoh had admitted sinning against the God of the Hebrews, Moses and Aaron felt Pharaoh would now give in. Instead he complained of some seeming conspiracy on the part of Moses and Aaron and the Israelites. Pharaoh thought only the men would leave to worship, and the women and children would stay. Since having all leave was not acceptable to Pharaoh, he had his servants drive Moses and Aaron away from his throne.

God then said to Moses, "Stretch your hand over the land of Egypt that locusts may invade it and devour all the vegetation in it." Then a strong East wind came up without end. At dawn, the East wind brought locusts. They swarmed over the entire land. Eventually, the land went black with locusts. They ate all the available vegetation in sight. At the same time, the locusts ate fruit remaining after the hail. No green vegetation remained throughout Egypt.

Pharaoh quickly called Moses and Aaron. He admitted having sinned against God and them. He asked for forgiveness and an end to the plague. Moses prayed to the Lord to relent. God switched to a strong West wind and blew all the locusts into the Red Sea. Still, Pharaoh remained stubborn.

# CROSSING THE RED SEA

*Exodus 12:29-36; 14:1-31*

THE last plague in which all firstborn of both men and animals were killed forced Pharaoh to let the Israelites go. Moses and Aaron were called to Pharaoh at night and Pharaoh said, "Leave at once." They were all allowed to leave with their flocks and herds.

After 430 years of captivity, 600,000 Israelites set out from Rameses. They avoided the Philistine lands lest they would have to fight. God thought they might give up and go back to Egypt, so He sent them toward the Red Sea through the desert. During the day, God went before them as a column of cloud, so they would know the way. At night, a column of fire would lead and give light. These columns never left the people and gave them great hope.

Later God told Moses where to camp near the Red Sea. God knew Pharaoh had his spies watching the Israelite migration. God told Moses that Pharaoh would think the Israelites were wandering around the desert as if lost. God planned to make Pharaoh go after the Israelites in order to force them back to Egypt.

Pharaoh regretted having let the Israelites go. With hundreds of

50

chariots filled with soldiers, Pharaoh went after the Israelites. The Israelites saw the dust of the approaching Egyptians and cried out against God. The people became very angry with Moses. He replied, "Fear not. Stand your ground, and you will secure victory. The Lord will win for you today."

God told Moses to lift his staff and stretch his arm to split the Red Sea. Darkness covered the area, and the Egyptians halted. All night a strong East wind came and parted the waters, drying a path. Once the people safely reached the other side, Pharaoh and his chariots followed. Their chariot wheels became clogged. Moses stretched out his hand and the sea rushed back. All of Pharaoh's forces were drowned. Seeing this, the people were struck with fear of the Lord and deepened their faith.

# MANNA IN THE DESERT

*Exodus 15:22—16:36*

FOLLOWING the destruction of Pharaoh's armies, Moses led the Israelites away to the desert of Shur. However, after three days' travel, the people discovered they could not drink the bitter waters of the desert area. Hearing their complaints, God told Moses to throw a certain kind of wood into the waters and they turned fresh. After a brief stop there, the Israelites moved toward Elim where there were a dozen wells and many palm trees.

The Israelite community then moved into the desert of Sin, located between Elim and Sinai. While in the desert, the community as a whole began to grumble against Moses and Aaron. Since food was in short supply, the people said they would have rather died in Egypt at the hand of God than starve to death in the desert. They talked of how in Egypt they reclined near their roasted meat fires, while having as much bread as they wanted. Moses and Aaron were not able to answer right away. They urged them not to give up hope, as things would get better as they neared their final destination.

God was aware of the people's grumblings. He told Moses that He would "rain down food from heaven." Moses was to instruct the people to go out early in the morning and collect enough food for the day. God wanted to test them to see if they would follow His instructions. On the sixth day, a double amount was to be collected so enough would be available in their tents during the Sabbath.

Moses and Aaron addressed the people and reminded them that when they grumbled against Moses and Aaron, they were really complaining against the Lord. Moses then told Aaron to have the entire Israelite community present themselves to God. They turned toward the desert and the glory of God appeared as a cloud. God spoke to Moses, saying He had heard the people's grumblings. Moses was to tell the people that at twilight there would be flesh meat to eat, and in the morning plenty of bread would be available as before.

The next evening the quail covered the camp. In the morning, a dew covered the camp. And when it dried it left flakes "like hoar frost" on the ground. At first, the people did not know what it was until Moses said, "This is the bread that the Lord has given us to eat."

The people called the food "manna." To them it looked like coriander seed. It dried into wafer-like pieces and was very sweet. In order to record God's blessings for their descendants, they gathered about one-tenth bushel of manna and preserved it.

# WATER FROM THE ROCK

*Exodus 17:1-7*

DESPITE their desert experience, it was important that the Israelites and their descendants remembered the food God provided. It became an important part of their history. Moses, at God's suggestion, had the preserved manna put in a golden vessel called an urn. Aaron placed the urn in front of two stone tablets of Commandments.

Until the Israelites arrived at permanent lands, they ate manna for forty years. They then reached the borders of Canaan. Eventually, they camped at Rephidim as God had commanded. However, there was no water there for the people to drink. They shouted angrily at Moses, "Give us water." Moses answered, "Why do you grumble against me? Why do you challenge the Lord?"

They wanted to know why Moses made them leave Egypt. They unfairly implied Moses led them to the desert to die of thirst, along with their children and livestock. The Israelites saw their flocks and herds as a guarantee of their physical survival in new lands. Their children were, in their minds, the most important foundation of their future community.

Moses was convinced he had to cry out to God. "What shall I do with this people? They are not far from stoning me." God heard Moses' cry. He was to gather as many people as possible, with all the elders of Israel. Taking his staff, God told Moses He would be standing on a rock in Horeb. "Strike the rock and water will come out of it." The place was called Massah and Meribah. Massah, a Hebrew word, means "a place of the test." Meribah means "the place of quarreling." The people and Moses had quarreled there, and questioned whether the Lord was with them. Still God did not punish them.

God allowed water to flow in great quantities. However, even though the need for water was met abundantly, below the surface, in their minds and hearts, the burning issue remained as to whether or not they should have left Egypt. They had left behind most of their possessions in Egypt, a place were many had lived all their lives. Except for Joseph, whose bones were carried with them, the remains of their loved ones and ancestors were left in a foreign land. Their faith had been sorely tested.

# ISRAELITES VICTORIOUS AGAINST AMALEK

*Exodus 17:8-16*

WHILE it is true that the Israelites were moving toward a promised land, still they had suffered shortages of food and water. Other more difficult challenges awaited them.

News of the great Israelite migration spread as they journeyed toward the final destination. While still at Rephidim, Amalek and his armies attacked the Israelites. Amalek was the leader of the Amalekites who were an aboriginal people of southern Palestine and the Sinai peninsula. In this instance, Moses relied on his personal leadership skills. He did not, for example, call upon the Lord, although he knew the Lord was watching over the Israelites.

Moses ordered Joshua to pick a group of elite men and organize them into a force capable of defending the Israelites. They were to begin at dawn of the first day after Amalek's attack. Moses promised Joshua he would be standing on a piece of high ground where he could observe the coming battle, while "holding the staff of God in my hand."

Joshua did as Moses told him. Aaron and Hur were also with Moses. They soon discovered that as long as Moses kept his hands raised, the Israelites succeeded in battle. When he let his arms rest, the Amalekites began to win the day. Moses became very tired, and a stone was placed for him to sit. Meanwhile, Aaron and Hur supported Moses' arms on either side. This allowed Moses to remain with hands raised until sunset. The battle turned in Israel's favor, and Joshua cut down Amalek and a great number of his people.

The Amalekite defeat came through Moses' determination to remain steadfast in prayer, despite his pain. With the battle over, and Moses having lived up to the demands of his leadership position, God spoke to him. The Lord told Moses to keep a record of the events and, at the same time, whisper to Joshua, "I will utterly blot out all memory of Amalek from under heaven."

In thanksgiving, Moses built an altar at the place of the battle. He called the altar Yahweh-nissi, which means, "the Lord is my banner." Following Amalek's challenge, the Israelites were more determined to move forward under the protection of the Lord.

# THE TEN COMMANDMENTS

*Exodus 19:1—20:22*

THREE months after the Israelites left Egypt, having left Rephidim, God's people camped in the Sinai desert at the foot of God's mountain, Mount Sinai. God called Moses and told him to remind the house of Jacob how the Lord guided them to Mount Sinai with care. The Lord also wanted the people to know if they kept His covenant and listened to Him they would be His special people. "I will count you as a kingdom of priests, a holy nation." Since the entire house of Jacob was consecrated to God in a special way, they were a race of "royal" priests who cooperated in offering sacrifice to God.

Responding to Moses, the people proclaimed, "All the Lord has spoken we will do." Then God told Moses to have the people prepare themselves for the third day by washing their garments. They then would see God come down to Mount Sinai. And God warned the people not to go up the mountain or even touch its base. If any man or animal did so, they would not be allowed to live.

When the third day arrived, great peals of thunder and lightning flashes shook the people. Then a cloud covered the mountain. And a trumpet blast was so frightening that the people trembled. When God arrived on top of Mount Sinai, He called Moses to come to Him. When Moses obeyed, God again told Moses to warn the people about not attempting to go up. Moses told God they understood His previous command. God said, "Go down now. Then come up again with Aaron."

God gave Moses and Aaron the Commandments. The laws were written in such a way that they imposed a command on individuals. One was told under obligation to either perform or not do some action. Aside from the first three Commandments, the remainder were originally a form of tribal wisdom. The elders of the tribe took their role seriously and did their best to provide for the common good.

The body of God's laws seem to be an intimate conversation between God and individual. God led His people out of Egypt, so "you shall not have other gods but Me." God's name was not to be spoken in vain. The Sabbath was to be holy. People were to honor fathers and mothers. Killing and adultery were forbidden. God's people were not to steal. Also, "You shall not give false evidence against your neighbor." One should not desire anything belonging to a neighbor. Finally, God told Moses, "Thus shall you speak to the children of Israel: You yourselves have seen that I have spoken to you from heaven."

# THE ANGER OF MOSES

*Exodus 32:15-35*

AFTER God had finished giving Moses the Commandments on Mount Sinai, He gave Moses two tablets of stone. On these tablets God had written the Commandments with His finger. Moses then planned his trip back down the mountain to bring God's law to His people.

Meanwhile, the Israelites were becoming impatient with Moses' long delay. Many had lost confidence in Moses' leadership. Protesting to Aaron that they did not know what happened to Moses, they asked for a different god to worship.

Aaron told the people to bring all their gold jewelry from which he made a golden calf. People proclaimed, "This is your God, O Israel, who rescued you from the land of Egypt." Aaron then built an altar in front of the calf and announced the following day as a "Feast of the Lord." Early the following morning, people brought all kinds of offerings to their new god. Then they acted shamefully.

God told Moses to hurry back to the Israelites, informing him of all they had done. God was very angry with His people. Moses begged God not to destroy them. After all that had been accomplished so far in the migration, if God destroyed the Israelites, His enemies would mock Him.

As Moses neared the camp he heard the drunken revelry. In anger he threw the tablets to the ground. He questioned Aaron as to why he built the calf. Aaron said that Moses knew the stubbornness of his people. Moses realized that Aaron had allowed the people to run wild. Moses called upon all the people who were with the Lord to gather. All the Levites backed Moses, and he ordered them to slay all in the camp who turned from God, about three thousand.

Moses called for an assembly of the people. He scolded them for having sinned gravely against God. He promised to return to God and ask forgiveness. Moses told God he would give up his salvation if the Lord relented. But God said, "Whoever has sinned against Me will I erase from My book." Moses was ordered back to the camp to lead the people to their final goal guided by an Angel of God, and God said, "When it is time for Me to punish, I will bring punishment upon them." In all his pleading with God, Moses was not disloyal to the Lord, but assured an unbroken line in humanity's history.

# THE ISRAELITES PREPARE TO ENTER CANAAN

*Numbers 13:1—14:38*

WITH their spirits lifted due to God's forgiveness of their great sin near Mount Sinai, the Israelite community moved on once more. After some time, they camped in the desert of Paran, at Kadesh. The Lord told Moses to send out men to explore the land He had planned for them. One man from each of the twelve ancestral tribes was sent. Hosea, son of Nun, one of the twelve, changed his name to Joshua at Moses' request. Hosea and Joshua come from one original name meaning "the Lord saves."

Moses told his scouts, "Go up into the Negeb, then into the highlands and see what the land is like." The Negeb was a dry area south of Judah. From there it was easier to move into the highlands of central Canaan. South of Jerusalem, by about twenty miles, stood the city of Horeb. The scouts reached there in a short time. They heard the area was famous for its grapes, pomegranates and figs. The place was known as the Wadi Eschol, "the valley of the cluster." Moses asked his scouts to determine the kinds of fruits available. And they happened to be there during the time of the grape harvest.

However, Moses was interested in more than just fruit. He wanted information on woodlands; the

quality of the soil for farming and grazing; the attractiveness for living conditions; size of the towns and whether or not they were fortified. Finally, the culture and customs of the people were to be part of their report. After forty days' exploration, the scouts were to return and explain their findings to Moses, Aaron and the whole community. At first there was favorable news of a land flowing "with milk and honey." This, of course, was the traditional description of the promised land.

Going from joy and anticipation, the scouts' findings moved to caution and reality. They determined the people were tall and strong descendants of the Anakim. The Anakim were known to be a numerous and fierce people. Before entering their area, the Israelites would have to defeat them. In general, it was a mixed population there consisting of Amalekites, Hittites, Jebusites, Amorites and Canaanites.

Finally, the searchers recommended the Israelites give up any notion of going into the promised land. Many felt they would never overcome the powerful communities there. Only Caleb raised his voice in support of going on, saying to the people hc knew they would be successful. But the entire community grumbled against Moses and Aaron at the news. Again, the people voiced their regrets at having left Egypt and were angry with God.

# MOSES RAISES THE BRASS SERPENT

*Numbers 21:1-9*

THE Canaanite king of Arad attacked and took some of the Israelites captive. The Israelites begged God to deliver Arad's forces into their hands and free their captured brothers. The Lord answered their request, and the Canaanites were scattered.

From Mount Hor, near Kadesh, the Israelites took the Red Sea road and bypassed the land of Edom. Since this was the longer way, the people began to lose patience and complained against God and Moses.

Almost immediately, God punished the people for their complaining by sending seraphs or poisonous serpents throughout the camp. Known for their fiery and painful bites, the serpents were responsible for many deaths. In a short time, the people came to Moses and admitted they had sinned against God and Moses. They asked Moses to pray to the Lord that the serpents might be driven away.

Moses accepted their request and the Lord responded favorably. God told Moses to make a seraph image of brass and put it on a pole. Anyone who had been bitten and looked at the brass serpent soon would be healed. Once Moses raised the image on the pole, those who looked at it were cured just as God had promised.

Events such as this were repeated over and over again. First, there would be rebellion, followed by a threat of punishment. Then came intercession with God, usually through Moses. Forgiveness was bestowed on the people time and time again. It seems the younger generation, over time, failed to learn a lesson about not raising complaints against Moses and the Lord when things became difficult.

Even though the next generation was beginning to mature, complaints remained the order of the day, especially when food and water were scarce, while, at the same time, expressing a desire to return to Egypt.

In the case of the brass serpent, there was a special message. To be cured, the people looked at an image of the creature that harmed them. Still, in their desire for a cure, in obedience and faith, they did what had to be done. This was to be another time the rebel Israelites, while on migration, would be forgiven.

# BALAAM AND THE ANGEL

*Numbers 22:22—23:12*

THE Israelites' long journey from Sinai to the Plains of Moab covered a generation. The people who survived gathered near Moab for the purposes of organizing themselves into a community of worshipers. They professed deep faith in the presence of God among them. This was the foundation of their belief. Still, even in this final stage before entering the promised land, enemies abounded.

Balak, the king of Moab, had grave fears over the thousands of Israelites gathering near his borders. He knew the Israelites had defeated the Amorites, whose army had defeated Balak's forces. He was angry at the growing numbers of Israelites who, in his estimation, "cover the face of the earth." At that time, many of Israel's neighbors probably felt the same way.

In his fear of the Israelites, Balak sent for Balaam. He believed that if Balaam, who was a soothsayer and fortune teller, forecast an evil omen for Israel, the evil would come about as if by magic. At the same time, Balak suggested to the Midianites that the Israelites could be very destructive and might well turn on Midian.

Balaam was a man of God and asked Him how he should answer Balak's messengers. God told Balaam not to go with the messengers and not to curse Israel, because "they are blessed." Balak sent messengers a second time. Balaam told them that even if given much gold and silver for pronouncing a curse, he would not do it since that would be against God's command. In the night, God came to Balaam and told him he could go with the messengers, but only on the condition that Balaam did exactly what God told him to do.

The next day Balaam saddled his donkey and went with the messengers. God's anger flared up since Balaam was putting himself in temptation's way because of his greed. God sent an Angel to the road Balaam was following. The donkey saw the Angel with a drawn sword and went off the side of the road. Balaam beat her back onto the road. A second time the donkey saw the Angel in a very narrow section, and it squeezed against the wall. It was beat back again. A third time the donkey saw the Angel and cowered under Balaam.

God gave the donkey a voice and it asked Balaam why he had

beat him three times. Balaam said if he had a sword he would kill the beast. God then allowed Balaam to see the Angel. Falling to his knees, he said, "I have sinned against God." The Angel told him to go to Balak, "but you may say only what I shall tell you." Balak took Balaam to see the Israelites' tents.

Balaam had seven altars built there, and Balak heard Balaam bless, not curse, Israel three times.

# THE ISRAELITES ENTER THE PROMISED LAND

*Deuteronomy 34:1-12; Joshua 1:1—4:24*

MOSES went up to Mount Nebo where he could see all the promised lands. God said to Moses that He allowed him to see the promised land from afar. Moses was punished for his lack of faith in striking the rock at Kadesh twice before water flowed from it. Shortly after Moses saw the promised lands, he died at age one hundred twenty.

Joshua, son of Nun, became the Israelite leader. At the Jordan River, he asked the people to pray that all would go well when they crossed over into the new land. But before crossing, Joshua sent two spies into Jericho to determine how strong the people were there. However, the king of Jericho found out spies were among his people, and he sent soldiers to arrest them.

In Jericho, the two spies had gone to a public house run by a woman named Rahab. Rahab was aware that God was leading the Israelites into her homeland. Rahab was told by the king to put the spies out of her home. Instead she hid them. When soldiers came, she said the spies had been there and gone. Since she hid the spies on her roof, she asked for her family's safety when the Israelites arrived. Agreement in hand, she let the spies down and told them to go up into the hill country for three days. They followed her instruction and arrived safely back with the Israelites, announcing the news that it was safe to move into Jericho.

Joshua started the people moving. Priests carried the Ark of the Covenant right up to the water's edge, and the water parted. All the people crossed on dry land. The priests with the Ark of the Covenant remained motionless in the dry river bed until the entire nation of Israel crossed.

God told Joshua to gather twelve men to take twelve stones from the Jordan River, where the priests were standing with the Ark. The twelve stones represented the twelve tribes. Joshua told the men, "In the future, they will be a sign among you. When your children ask the meaning of these stones, you shall answer, 'The waters of the Jordan were stopped before the Ark of the Covenant of the Lord when it crossed the Jordan.' These stones are to serve as an everlasting reminder to the Israelites." Clearly, it was the Lord Who brought the Israelites across the Jordan.

# THE ARK OF THE COVENANT

*Exodus 25:1—26:36; Joshua 3:1-17; 4:7-11*

AS the Israelite community traveled toward the promised land, they carried with them many symbols of their beliefs, religion and political history. Still, while in exile, they sorely missed their temple, the very center of their worship.

The Lord told Moses to ask the Israelites to take up a collection for Him. They were to accept gold, silver and bronze; violet, purple and scarlet yarn; fine linens and goat hair; skins dyed red; porpoise skins; acacia wood; onyx stones, oil and incense. "You shall make a sanctuary for me."

The Ark was made of acacia wood. It was about sixty inches long, thirty inches wide and thirty-two inches high. It was plated inside and out with pure gold. A gold molding was placed around the top. There were four gold rings, two on each side, opposite one another. Gold-plated acacia wood poles were fitted through the rings, never allowed to be removed from the Ark, thus making the ark portable.

A pure gold propitiatory was molded as a cover for the ark. It was about sixty inches long and thirty inches wide. Two cherubim of beaten gold were placed at either end of the propitiatory. They took the form of human headed, winged lions. Wings spread over the Ark, the cherubim formed a throne for the invisible Lord.

An acacia-wood table provided a convenient resting place for worship functions. This table also had four rings and accompanying poles, and it was carried much the same way as the Ark. Moreover, there were plates, cups and pitchers of pure gold to be used in rituals.

The table held the showbread, or holy bread, placed on the table every Sabbath as an offering to God. It was later eaten by the priests. The cups held incense that was sprinkled over the bread. A menorah, or seven-branch candlestick of gold, completed the Ark.

In the Ark rested the two tablets of stone upon which were written God's Commandments. A golden urn of manna was added at Moses' command. In effect, the Ark was the holy of holies for the Israelites. Since it was portable, it moved with the people and was the center of their worship. It was God present to His people.

# THE WALLS OF JERICHO

*Joshua 5:13—6:27*

HAVING crossed the Jordan into the promised land, the Israelites camped at Gilgal, on the plains of Jericho. Passover was celebrated on the eve of the fourteenth day of the first month of the year. The next day the Israelites began to eat local food of unleavened cakes and parched grain. The following day manna did not appear in the camp, and from that time on the Israelites ate the produce of Canaan.

A few days later, while Joshua was near Jericho city, he saw an individual with sword in hand, who explained he was the captain of the Angel host of the Lord. Before the Angel would give Joshua God's message, he was told to remove his sandals, since the place where Joshua stood was holy. Because of the large Israelite presence, Jericho was in a siege-like mode. God told Joshua He had delivered Jericho and its king into Joshua's power. Joshua was to have all his soldiers march around the outside walls of Jericho for six days, with seven priests carrying rams' horns before the Ark of the Covenant. On the seventh day, all the priests would blow the rams' horns. That would be the signal for all the people to shout at the top of their voices. The walls would collapse, and the Israelites could make a frontal attack.

Joshua called together priests, people and soldiers and told them God's plan. Each of the first six days they did as God commanded until Joshua gave the signal. On the seventh day, they marched around the city seven times. The seventh time Joshua gave the signal, saying, "Shout, for the Lord is giving you the city."

Joshua gave orders that Rahab and all her household be spared. The people were not to take anything in their greed. Metals were collected, but only for the Lord's treasury. In conquering Jericho, they put the sword to all living creatures. Joshua sent the two spies to Rahab's house to rescue all her kin. Then they led Rahab's entire family to the outskirts of the Israelite camp. The city was burned with everything in it except the metals for the Lord's treasury.

That same day Joshua imposed an oath before the Lord on any man who attempted to rebuild Jericho. The Lord was with Joshua. His fame became worldwide. Rahab married Salmon of Judah's tribe and became the great-great grandmother of David, an ancestor of Christ.

# THE STRENGTH OF SAMSON

*Judges 13:1—14:7*

**D**URING Joshua's lifetime, and those of his elders who outlived him, Israel was, for the most part, faithful to God. Joshua died at the age of a hundred and ten. He was buried in the mountain region of Ephraim. Still many dangers remained for the Israelites in the promised land. It took a long time for the pagans to be overcome. Therefore, God continued to send leader-heroes for the people. Referred to as judges, they were usually military leaders who had to defend the Israelites at different times and places.

There were occasions when the people would begin to worship pagan gods, and God would punish them by allowing pagan forces to be victorious over them. When the people turned back to God in sorrow, He would give them a great leader to save them from pagan forces and injustices. One of the great judges was Samson.

Manoah, whose wife was unable to have children, longed for a son. Hearing Manoah's prayers, God sent an Angel to his wife and told her she would have a son. She was warned not to drink wine, and to eat nothing unclean according to the law. Her son was to be consecrated from the womb. The word consecrated comes from the Hebrew word "nazir." Samson therefore was to be under the nazirite vow for life, meaning he would be obliged to abstain from drinking wine, and his hair was never to be cut by razor.

Manoah felt slighted that he and his wife were not together when the Angel visited, so the Angel returned. Manoah asked the Angel his name. He answered, "Why do you ask me my name, which is secret?" This implied that the Angel was speaking to Manoah and his wife in the name of the Lord Himself.

After Samson's birth he grew up strong and was blessed by God. As a powerful young adult, he did not hesitate to wrestle and kill wild beasts with his bare hands. Despite his great physical strength, Samson never gathered or led an army of his own. It was as if in the minds of the Philistines Samson was the local bully. They did not like Samson, and they resented his presence among them.

Yet, they were aware of his attachment to the Israelite God, and that he would always stand by the Israelites. Well aware of the stories of his killing beasts without armor, they planned to get rid of him some way.

# SAMSON AND DELILAH

*Judges 14:19—16:15*

LIKE several of the hero-judges of his day, Samson was not without his faults. He was known to have broken his nazirite vows. At times he seemed to be controlled by lust. He would use his God-given, special, personal strength to take revenge on his enemies. Once, he slew one thousand men with the jawbone of a donkey. When the Philistines threatened to kill his wife, Samson went down to Ashkelon and killed thirty men there.

After some time away, Samson went to visit his wife. But his father-in-law would not allow him into his home. He thought Samson had left his daughter for good, so he gave Samson's wife to his good friend and best man from the first marriage. Samson promised revenge on his father-in-law and the Philistines. He caught three hundred foxes and tied a torch between each pair of tails. He lit the torches and sent the foxes through Philistine grain fields. Vineyards and olive groves were set afire by the blazing grain. When the Philistines found Samson out, they destroyed his first wife and her family. Meanwhile, Samson settled in a cave in the cliffs of Etam. Despite all his excesses, God provided for him.

Once in Gaza, Samson was attracted to and became friendly with a woman of ill repute. When local men found out Samson was at her house, they prepared to ambush him at the city gates to kill him. But, at midnight, Samson took the doors and the posts of the city gates and tore them loose. No one dared lay a hand on him.

Later Samson fell in love with Delilah. Aware of their relationship, Philistine leaders went to Delilah and asked her to try to discover the secret of Samson's strength. For her aid, Delilah would be paid eleven shekels of silver. Delilah agreed.

She asked Samson how he could be tied to be made helpless. He told her seven fresh, dried bowstrings would do it. The Philistines gave her the bowstrings wet, and she tied him. She told him the Philistines had come. He snapped the bowstrings. Delilah pretended to be hurt because Samson would not tell his secret. Samson said if she wove seven locks of his hair and fastened them with a pin, he would turn weak. As he slept, she wove and pinned his hair. When he awoke, he pulled out the pin. Delilah cried that Samson mocked her by his actions. Her efforts to find the secret went on.

# SAMSON REGAINS HIS STRENGTH

Judges 16:16-31

SAMSON continued to live with Delilah despite her constant complaints that he would not give up his secret. Samson finally gave in and agreed to take Delilah into his confidence. He told Delilah that he had been consecrated to God since birth, by vow, and his head had never been touched by a razor. If he shaved his head he would lose his strength.

Delilah called the lords of the Philistines to come to her place. They were to bring the money. Delilah had Samson asleep on her lap. One of the men cut off his hair. When she told him the Philistines were there he jumped up. He tried to escape as he had done previously. God's power had left him, and it took him a minute to understand.

The Philistines subdued him and gouged out his eyes. Then he was taken to Gaza and bound in bronze chains. Treated like an ordinary prisoner, Samson was sent to the prison grist mill. But, as soon as he had been shaved, his hair began to grow again. In their great glee at Samson's capture, they overlooked his new hair.

Later, the Philistines assembled all their important people. They offered a sacrifice to the god Dagon. Following the sacrificial rite, they began celebrating, chanting, "Our god has delivered Samson our enemy into our hands." As they drank more and more, they decided to bring Samson to their temple in order to make sport of him. When he was brought in, the people praised their god for having delivered their enemy, "the man who has laid our country to waste."

Samson asked to be placed between the two main temple columns to support himself against them. All the Philistine lords were there with their families, and about three thousand more were watching the festivities. Samson cried out to the Lord to restore his power in order to avenge the loss of his eyes. Grasping both columns he prayed to the Lord, "Let me die with the Philistines." Then he pushed with all his strength and the temple collapsed, killing more people at his death than he had during his life.

His family recovered the body. Samson was buried beside his father. Through Samson, God carried out His designs for His people.

# RUTH

*Ruth 1:1—4:17*

RUTH, like Samson, is one of the prominent ancestors of the Israelites. In contrast to Samson, her story is a pleasant tale of love and devotion to family and neighbor. Understanding their roots helped many in Israel to live uprightly in accord with God's wishes.

Ruth lived in a nation that suffered much during the time of the judges. Many experienced painful hunger. Her in-laws, for example, were desperately poor and had to move with their two sons from Bethlehem of Judah to the pagan land of Moab. While there, their two sons married Moab women.

The husband and sons of her mother-in-law Naomi died. She decided to move back to Bethlehem. She wanted her two daughters-in-law to return to their families, where they might find new husbands and happiness among the Moab men.

One accepted Naomi's plan, but Ruth did not. She did not want Naomi to be alone and went with her, saying, "Your people will be my people, your God will be my God." Arriving in Bethlehem, Naomi and Ruth found conditions quite difficult. Fortunately, some landowners would allow poor people to scour their lands after harvest. That way they could gather grains left on the ground by field hands. Ruth volunteered to go and find food for Naomi and herself. It was backbreaking and humiliating work, but it prevented starvation.

Ruth was working in the fields owned by Boaz. On an inspection tour, he noticed Ruth and admired her work and beauty. He asked his foreman about her. He then told her she was welcome to gather leftovers anytime. Moreover, he told his workers to make sure there was enough grain dropped for Ruth and Naomi to survive.

Ruth told Naomi what happened. Naomi was delighted since she knew Boaz to be a distant cousin. Rather boldly, Naomi told Ruth to go back to Boaz's tent that evening, and sleep at his feet. When Boaz saw her the next day, he decided to marry Ruth.

However, a relative, according to strict law, had first right to have her in marriage. Before the elders of the city, Boaz asked his intentions about Ruth. He was not interested, so Boaz married her. They were blessed by God with a son, Obed. He would become the great-grandfather of King David.

# THE CHILD SAMUEL

*1 Samuel 1:1—3:18*

FROM time to time, groups of the Israelite community would turn away from God. Eventually, they would turn back to Him. Their forgiving God would give them both another chance and a new leader or judge. The final judge in Israel was Samuel.

Samuel's father, Elkanah, a Zuphite from the hills of Ephraim, had two wives. One had many children, but Hannah had none. She dearly wanted a son. During many temple visits, with copious tears, she implored God for a child. Eli, a priest, heard her wailing. Hannah told him her loud, tearful prayers came from the depths of her heart because she had no son. Eli said, "Go in peace. May the God of Israel answer your prayer."

In a short time, Hannah conceived and had a son called Samuel. She intended to give Samuel back to God "to be His forever." Once Samuel was old enough to be away from home, she took him to the temple at Shiloh. Through Eli, Samuel was presented to the Lord and left at the temple. He would remain there in the Lord's service.

One day Eli was sleeping in his temple alcove alone. Samuel tried to stay awake since the sanctuary lamp was still lit, but he fell asleep near the Ark. The Lord called Samuel, and he answered, "Here I am," and ran to Eli. Eli was disturbed and said he had not called, and Samuel should go back to sleep. When this happened for a third time, Eli began to suspect the hand of the Lord was involved. Therefore, he told Samuel if he heard the call again he should simply answer, "Speak, Lord, for your servant is listening." Samuel went back to sleep and the Lord called again. He answered as Eli instructed.

The Lord revealed to Samuel there would be great concerns in Israel. In addition, the Lord swore that no sacrifice or offering would ever make up for their crimes.

God left Samuel, and the young man went back to sleep. The next day, after opening the temple doors, Samuel was afraid to tell Eli about the vision. But Eli called Samuel and asked, "What message did He give you?" Eli warned Samuel not to hide anything, or God would punish him. So Samuel told all. Eli said, "He is the Lord. He will do what is good." Eli had taught Samuel the necessity of being open and ready to listen to God.

# THE PHILISTINES SEIZE THE ARK

*1 Samuel 4:1—7:14*

THE Philistines mounted an attack against Israel. The Israelite armies met the enemy at Ebenezer. A great battle followed, and Israel was defeated. Nearly four thousand were lost on the battlefield. Following the battle, the leaders of the Israelites met and wondered why the Lord allowed their defeat. For more assistance they decided to bring the Ark of the Covenant from Shiloh to take into the next battle.

Arrangements were made to transport the Ark from Shiloh to Ebenezer. Eli's two sons accompanied the Ark. When the Ark came into camp at Ebenezer the people shouted so loudly it grabbed the Philistines' attention. Hearing the Ark was now with the Israelites, the Philistines became frightened. They remembered it was Israel's God Who had led their people out of Egypt. Now they feared the same God would destroy or weaken them. They could suffer defeat and be enslaved by the Israelites.

The Philistines rallied their forces. A massive battle began between the two nations. The Philistines were victorious, and the remaining Israelites fled to their tents, having lost thirty thousand foot soldiers that day. But the worst tragedy was the Philistines' capture of the Ark of the Covenant.

A Benjaminite was able to flee the battle scene and get to Shiloh. Eli, sitting in his temple seat, barely saw him enter Shiloh, covered with dirt, with his clothes in shreds. Eli worried all day about the Ark. Eli heard a cry in the city and asked the meaning of it. On hearing of the defeat of the Israelites and the death of his sons, he fell backward from his chair and died from a broken neck.

The Philistines took the Ark and placed it in Dagon's temple. The next day, Dagon was found prostrate before the Ark. The next morning, his head and hands were broken off and lying on the temple threshold. Later the Philistines carried the Ark to different towns. In each place the people suffered a pestilence and were over run with mice. The people begged the elders to send the Ark back to the Israelites. After seven months, priests and fortune-tellers were asked how to send the Ark back. They returned the Ark to Beth-shemesh with a guilt offering. There it was placed on a large stone in the field of Joshua.

# SAMUEL ANOINTS SAUL

*1 Samuel 7:15—10:1*

SAMUEL judged Israel for forty years. Every year he visited his people in Bethel, Gilgal and Mizpah, establishing good order where needed. Then he would return home to Ramah.

As he grew older, Samuel appointed his sons judges. Joel and Abijah judged at Beer-sheba. They were a disappointment. As a result, all the elders of Israel met with Samuel at Ramah. They asked Samuel to appoint a king so they could be like other nations. Though unhappy with their request, he prayed to the Lord for guidance. God explained that the people were not rejecting Samuel, but the Lord.

God noted that since the people had been released from slavery in Egypt, they had been deserting Him and worshiped strange gods. Still, God told Samuel to give them what they wanted. At the same time, Samuel was to warn and inform the people of the rights of a ruler-king.

Samuel informed the people of a king's rights. Young men could be taken to serve the king's chariots and horses. Some would become commanders of thousands of men. Others could be told to plow, harvest fields and make weapons and chariot parts.

Women would become cooks, bakers and cosmetic makers. They would be taxed one-tenth of all income. And one tenth of all slaves and animals would be required by a king. Despite all this, the people demanded a king. When God saw this, he told Samuel, "Listen to their appeal and appoint a king over them."

The elders returned to their home cities in search of a king. A Benjaminite named Kish had a son named Saul, who was known for his good looks and tall bearing. In a search for his father's lost donkeys, Saul asked a man of God for advice and help. On the way to his city, they encountered Samuel. The Lord told Samuel he would meet a Benjaminite "whom you are to anoint as ruler of My people," and their savior from the Philistines.

Saul asked Samuel the whereabouts of a local prophet. He answered, "I am a seer," meaning prophet. Samuel entertained Saul and gave him a place to sleep. At dawn, Samuel asked to speak with Saul alone. "I have a message to give you from God." Samuel poured a bottle of oil over Saul's head. He kissed him saying, "The Lord appoints you ruler over His heritage."

# SAUL DISOBEYS GOD

*1 Samuel 15:1-35*

AFTER becoming king of Israel, Saul engaged many of Israel's enemies in battle. It seemed wherever he carried his wars he was victorious. And he was known for his personal bravery. He waged an unremitting war against the Philistines during his lifetime. At home, if he became aware of any young man of great strength and bravery, Saul recruited him for his military organization.

Once Samuel spoke to Saul and reminded Saul that it was Samuel who had anointed him king of Israel. Samuel gave Saul a message from God. God wanted Amalek punished for all he had done to Israel as its people wandered the desert toward the promised land. Amalek and his forces were to be put under the ban, meaning all people and things were to be exterminated. Nothing could be reserved for private use.

Saul then gathered two hundred thousand soldiers, and ten thousand men of Judah and, after allowing the Kenites to escape the city of Amalek, he attacked with all his fury, establishing with his people beforehand the dreaded ban. All the Amalekites and their flocks were put to the sword. But Saul took Agag, king of Amalek, alive, and spared the best of the animals.

God then said to Samuel that He regretted having made Saul king, since he disobeyed His command. Saul saw Samuel approach and said, "May you be blessed! I have kept the Lord's command." Samuel asked why he heard animals making noise. Samuel then told Saul what the Lord said, and asked why Saul had disobeyed the Lord by not fulfilling the ban. Saul said, "I brought back Agad, and I destroyed Amalek." Saul, realizing Samuel's visit was at God's direction, began to see that he had offended the Lord.

Saul admitted his sin. He asked Samuel to return with him to worship the Lord together. Samuel refused. Worst of all, Samuel told Saul, "The Lord has rejected you as king over Israel."

As Samuel turned to go, Saul grabbed a loose end of Samuel's cloak, tearing it. Samuel replied, "The Lord has torn the kingdom of Israel from you this day and given it to a neighbor of yours." Devastated and admitting his sin, Saul begged Samuel to worship God with him before the elders of Israel. For future unity, Samuel agreed.

# DAVID AND SAUL

*1 Samuel 16:1-23*

SAMUEL grieved over the downfall of Saul, but the Lord wanted Saul's successor appointed quickly. God told Samuel to go to Bethlehem, where he was to be in touch with Jesse. The Lord had chosen one of Jesse's sons to succeed Saul. Samuel was afraid to set out for Bethlehem, since if Saul discovered the plan, he would kill him. But God told Samuel to take a heifer to sacrifice, and invite Jesse and his family to the sacrificial feast. This would remove any suspicions of Saul.

The Bethlehem elders feared Samuel's visit would not be peaceful. They were satisfied when Samuel told them of the feast. All Jesse's sons were to be there so Samuel could weigh their qualities as possible leaders. God warned Samuel, "Man looks at appearances, but the Lord sees the heart." Jesse presented seven sons, but none seemed right to Samuel.

Samuel asked if Jesse had other sons. He had one named David who was tending sheep. Jesse sent for him. "He was ruddy, had beautiful eyes and made a handsome appearance." The Lord told Samuel to anoint David, and he did so in the presence of his brothers. After the anointing, Samuel returned to Ramah.

Meanwhile, Saul, still technically king, fell into deep melancholy. Saul believed he was tormented by an evil spirit since the spirit of the Lord had left him. His worried servants asked Saul's permission to seek out a musician for him to make him feel better. Saul asked if a skilled harpist was available. One servant knew one of Jesse's sons played the harp well, was a good soldier, an effective speaker and handsome. He said further, "The Lord is with him."

Right away Saul sent his messengers to Jesse and asked him to send David. David thus entered Saul's service and Saul was fond of him, making David his armor-bearer. Saul later asked Jesse to allow David to stay with him.

David's playing made Saul's melancholy disappear. At first, Saul and David got along well. David's role as armor-bearer was really training in preparation for kingship. David and Saul became too close. Moreover, the relationship would eventually lead to a number of challenges for both men.

# DAVID AND GOLIATH

*1 Samuel 17:1-54*

THE Philistines and the Israelites came together to do battle in the Vale of the Terebinth. Camped on opposite hillsides, the champion Philistine, named Goliath, came out of the Philistine camp to show himself. Clad in bronze helmet and a bronze corset of armor, he stood six-and-a-half feet tall. He taunted the Israelites, asking why they appeared in battle formation. Then he threw down a challenge for the Israelites to choose one man to fight with Goliath alone. The winner's side would take all.

Meanwhile, David would come and go between his father's flocks and Saul's camp. His three brothers were also among Saul's warriors. Once Jesse packed up some food for his sons and gave it to David to take back. When David reached camp, they were moving out to battle the Philistines. David went to the front lines. While he was there, Goliath made another appearance.

In camp there was talk of a great reward for anyone who killed Goliath. When some soldiers spoke of the reward, David's interest grew. But his eldest brother Eliab became angry with him, demanding to know why David was in camp and not guarding the sheep. He scolded David for his scheming arrogance.

Hearing of the argument, Saul sent for David. Then David pledged his service to Saul and asked if he could fight Goliath. Saul said David was too young and inexperienced. David argued that when tending sheep he had killed both a lion and a bear. He knew that the Lord Who had delivered him from the ravages of the lion and bear would protect him from Goliath. Saul answered, "Go! May the Lord be with you."

Saul put his tunic and armor on David. The armor was too bulky, so he took it off. With only a staff in hand, he picked five smooth stones from the riverbed and put them in his shepherd's bag. David and Goliath advanced toward one another. Goliath shouted that he would leave David's flesh for the birds and animals. David responded that the Lord would deliver Goliath to him.

In an instant, David took a stone and shot it with his sling. It hit Goliath in the forehead and killed him. David ran to the body, took Goliath's sword and cut off his head. He held it high. The Philistines fled, with the Israelites and men of Judah in hot pursuit.

# DAVID ESCAPES FROM SAUL

*1 Samuel 18:6-30; 23:25—24:23*

FOLLOWING Goliath's slaying, when Saul and David were together and women from cities of Israel came to meet King Saul, they were singing and dancing. They played and sang, "Saul has killed his thousands, and David his ten thousands." From then on, Saul was jealous of David.

The following day, Saul was taken by an evil spirit while David was playing the harp. He took his spear and tried to thrust David through, but David escaped twice. Despite David's attempts to reconcile with Saul later, many plans were hatched in Saul's mind to kill David. He tried to nail David with a spear, but failed. Again, he sent David against the Philistines in a way in which he hoped David would be killed. Instead of killing one hundred Philistines as requested, David returned with evidence he had killed two hundred. This convinced Saul to give David his daughter Michal in marriage.

Despite the fact that David was now Saul's son-in-law, the king continued plans to kill him. Jonathan, Saul's son, and David became good friends. Both Jonathan and Michal decided to help David. Jonathan persuaded his father to swear not to kill David,

but, this had no effect. Michal convinced David he was in great danger. She let him down through a window to safety and cleverly misled her father's soldiers. They failed to capture David.

David hid himself among the prophets of Ramah. Saul and his messengers went there to get David, but they were taken by the spirit of the Lord, and in the eyes of the people they seemed foolish to pursue David. God was protecting David, and this became a major source of discomfort and frustration for Saul.

David continued to hide out. In a cave near the Dead Sea, one night Saul arrived and bedded down, unaware of David's presence. While Saul slept, David cut a piece from Saul's cloak. The next day Saul realized David spared him. Again, David caught Saul asleep and removed his spear and water bottle. Saul heard David and called him. David asked Saul why he was chasing him, since he had done nothing wrong. Saul, admitting his sinfulness, asked David to return. "When the Lord delivered me into your grasp you did not kill me. May the Lord now reward you generously." The two then parted in peace.

# THE DEATH OF SAUL

*1 Samuel 31—2 Samuel 1:1-10*

IT was not long before the Philistines again attacked Israel. When Saul realized the size and strength of the Philistines, he was afraid and prayed for guidance. However, he received no answer. In desperation, he went to a fortune-teller, a witch. When she asked whom he wanted to call from the dead, he said Samuel. When the witch saw an old man, Saul bowed to the ground. Samuel asked him why he had disturbed him.

Saul told Samuel of the growing numbers and fierceness of the Philistines and their plan to attack Israel. Samuel reminded Saul he had been rejected by the Lord. He recalled how some time before he had been warned that his kingdom would go to David. Further, since Saul disobeyed the Lord, the next day Saul would be with Samuel and his sons. At this response, Saul fainted from weakness and fear.

When the witch saw Saul faint she revived and helped him. She reminded Saul that at one time she had to obey him as king. Now he must obey her. He ate a feast of fatted calf she had prepared. It turned out to be Saul's last banquet.

As a great battle erupted, the Philistines charged Saul and his sons, keeping them in their sights. Jonathan, Abinadab and Malchishua, Saul's sons, were slain in his sight. As the battle intensified, Saul found himself surrounded. Philistine archers pierced Saul's abdomen.

Then Saul told his armor-bearer, "Draw your sword and pierce me through, so these uncircumcised may not come and make sport of me." At first, his armor-bearer refused since he was so frightened. So Saul took his own sword and fell on it, mortally wounding himself. When his armor-bearer saw what happened, he fell on his sword and died at Saul's side. That day saw the total devastation and end of Saul's regime.

The following day the Philistines came to strip the dead. They found Saul and his three sons lying almost together. They cut off Saul's head, and stripped him of his armor. Messengers were sent with news of victory throughout Philistine lands. There was great rejoicing among the people. Saul's armor was kept as a trophy and placed in the temple of Astarte. However, his body was hung on the wall of Bethshan.

# DAVID BECOMES KING

*2 Samuel 5:1-13*

WITH the house of Saul weakened, David's house became stronger and more numerous. With the defection of Abner from Saul's house to David's, all the tribes connected with Saul wanted to come over to David. However, David wanted his wife Michal returned before he would accept Abner coming over. This was the basis for their reconciliation. But Joab suspected Abner of treachery and tricked Abner into coming back to Hebron, where he killed Abner without David's permission. David's great distress over the death of Abner was seen in his funeral oration for Abner. The people realized David was not responsible for Abner's execution.

These events finally led to all the tribes of Israel coming to Hebron. They told David of his great accomplishments during Saul's reign. They recalled the Lord saying to David, "You shall be shepherd of My people Israel and ruler over Israel." David made an agreement in God's presence to become king. Then the elders anointed him as king of Israel. He was thirty years old at that time and would rule Israel for forty years.

Following his anointing, David and his forces moved against Jerusalem and the Jebusites who lived in that area. Jerusalem was known to be difficult to conquer due to its strong fortifications. Many believed at the time that the lame and the blind could easily defend it. Thus, the Jebusites chanted to David and his people, "You cannot come in here; the blind and the lame will prevent you." However, David easily took Zion's stronghold called the City of David. Jerusalem was indeed now a strong city with David's people streaming in there, and needed fortifications were established. But, most of all, God's spirit dwelt there with His people.

Meanwhile, Hiram, king of Tyre, sent overtures to David and provided a supply of cedarwood and a small army of carpenters and masons to build David's palace. In his awareness of all the Lord had done for him, David became more comfortable with the knowledge that he was indeed the king of Israel, and had been exalted by God for Israel's sake.

With his family settled in Jerusalem, David began to plan the future of Israel and knew he would be challenged.

# THE DEATH OF ABSALOM

*2 Samuel 14:25—15:12; 18:1-17*

ONE of the bright stars in King David's crown was his son Absalom. He was known throughout Israel for his good looks and well-trained body. He was endowed with an unusual crop of hair. Absalom was, to say the least, David's favorite son, and his love for him was without measure.

As Absalom grew older, he began to resent his father and started to plot against him. He would stand by the city gates and converse with people who had legal disputes to be settled by the king. Absalom would usually side with the claimant, and would say if he was appointed a judge, he would be available to render a favorable decision. Accordingly, Absalom's favorable reputation spread throughout Israel.

Some years later, Absalom asked permission of David to go to Hebron to fulfill a vow he made to God. The king gladly gave his blessing. Absalom sent messengers ahead to tell the people that when they heard trumpets to shout that he had been crowned king of Hebron.

The king soon heard of Absalom's plots. Even though the king was aware of Absalom's plans, thousands of Hebrews decided to follow Absalom. In view of all this, David told his people and ministers to flee Jerusalem, since he did not know what Absalom might do. He feared his son would attack Jerusalem and put to death the king and all his allies.

As the king left Jerusalem, his family and officials stopped opposite the ascent of the Mount of Olives. They watched the king's entire army pass in review. The people were distressed at the sight and wept. David told the priest Zadok to take back the Ark to the city. If the king found favor with God, He would bring David back and see the Ark in its proper place.

Absalom's rebellion deeply disturbed David. Acknowledging his sins and accepting God's will, David ordered his generals to fight Absalom. The king's son was soon defeated, and Absalom fled for his life.

Trying to get away from a group of David's soldiers, Absalom's hair was caught in a large tree. Since one of Joab's men refused to kill Absalom, Joab did it himself. Absalom's body was thrown into a deep pit and covered with rocks. Then all the Israelites fled.

# KING SOLOMON

*1 Kings 1:1-48; 3:1-28*

AS David grew older, the question the question of his successor often came up in the minds and hearts of his people. There were many behind-the-scenes movements among throne-seekers. One day, Bathsheba went to David and asked whom he planned to make his successor. She reminded him that he promised to make Solomon, their son, the next king. David agreed, but she argued that another of their sons had already claimed the throne.

This news angered David. He sent for Solomon to come at once to the palace. Immediately, Solomon was crowned king. Thus, David assured himself and all Israel that there would be no question over the succession, but Solomon was uneasy. He was very young. And he fully realized that he might not be able to succeed his father effectively. At once, he allied himself with Egypt by marrying the Pharaoh's daughter. Following that, he went to a very holy place and offered a thousand holocausts upon its altar.

That night God appeared to Solomon in a dream, and He promised to give him anything. Solomon replied, "O Lord, my God, You have made me, Your servant, king to succeed my father David; but I am a young man, unskilled in leadership." God was pleased with Solomon because he asked to know the right thing to do. God then blessed him with wisdom and understanding like no other person. "None to follow will compare with you." God also gave Solomon riches, glory and a long life. Returning to Jerusalem, Solomon sacrificed before the Ark, asking for peace and providing a feast for his servants.

Once two women came before Solomon with a difficult case. They lived together in the same house. One had given birth to a boy child that lived. Three days later, the other bore a child but he died. They brought a claim that the children had been switched at night. Thus, both women claimed the living child. The second woman denied all the first said and claimed to be mother of the child. Solomon asked for a sword. He ordered the child cut in two, and each woman to receive half. The real mother strongly objected. The other said, "It shall be neither mine nor yours; divide it." Solomon gave the baby to the real mother. All Israel was astounded at his wisdom in this.

# THE TRIUMPH OF SOLOMON

*1 Kings 6:1-38; 7:13-51*

SOLOMON'S reputation spread throughout the known world. People of many nations looked to him for greatness. He also became noted as a builder of many beautiful structures.

Just about four hundred and eighty years after Israel fled Egypt, and four years into his reign, Solomon began to build a great temple in Jerusalem. Although his father David had wanted to construct a temple, it was not God's will for him to do so. However, God approved Solomon's building plans, and he knew the temple would not confine the Lord. So, Solomon planned a magnificent temple.

Initially, Solomon, by treaty, sought the help of King Hiram of Tyre. Hiram would supply precious cedarwood, while Solomon would provide food for Hiram and his people. At the same time, Solomon arranged for some workers to cut huge blocks of stone from his quarries. This work as well as other kinds of crafts were performed at some distance from the temple so as to keep the temple land as sacred as possible.

Solomon's plan called for a building nearly ninety feet long, thirty feet wide and forty feet high. Outside, stone walls were covered with wood. Wooden rafters supported a wood roof. The completed building had flooring of inlaid fir planks. The holy of holies, at the rear of the building, was behind cedar partitions. The Ark of the Covenant would rest in the holy of holies. In front of the sanctuary was a forty-foot-long open worship space. Interior cedar walls of the temple had carved gourds and open flowers. The entire interior was overlaid with gold. A cedarwood altar, placed in front of the holy of holies, was also overlaid with gold.

In the holy of holies were two large olivewood cherubim, covered with gold. The floors of the inner and outer chambers were overlaid with gold. It took Solomon seven years to complete the temple. A number of precious furnishings were added.

During construction, God spoke to Solomon: "As to the temple you are building—if you walk in My statutes, obey My ordinances, and keep all My commandments, I will fulfill to you the promise I made to your father David. I will dwell among the Israelites and will not forsake My people Israel."

# THE PROPHET ELIJAH

*1 Kings 17:1—19:18*

FOLLOWING the death of Solomon in 930 B.C., Israel was divided into two sections. The Northern section was Israel, with Jeroboam as king. Judah was the South portion under king Rehoboam. Both areas became politically and economically weak. The following century began under King Ahab. He ruled in Samaria for twenty-two years. Ahab had a reputation of being evil. He married Jezebel, and, with her influence, he began to worship Baal. He erected an altar to Baal and allowed Jezebel to convince him to turn on the Lord's followers.

The Lord's prophet Elijah warned of a great drought in the land. It did not rain for three years, punishment for the people's turning to Baal. Elijah traveled north during the drought. Stopping at a widow's tent, he asked for a bit to eat. She said she had only enough for one meal for her child and herself. Elijah asked her to use what she had, and she obeyed. There was enough for the meal that day. Because she obeyed there would be enough food for her family until the drought's end.

The drought was so bad that the priests of Baal prayed, danced, shouted and cut themselves. Their god did not answer. Tired of pagan rites, Elijah stepped in and wet his sacrifice with water. He asked God to send fire on the offering so all would know the true God.

God's fire consumed the wet offering. People noticed, confessed they had sinned and prayed for forgiveness. Elijah said, "Seize the prophets of Baal. Do not let any of them escape!" Then he had all their throats slit.

Despite God's power worked through Elijah, he was forced to flee the anger and violence of Jezebel. Leaving his servant, he went a day's journey and rested beneath a broom tree. He asked God to take his life and fell asleep. An Angel touched him and told him to get up and eat. A hearth cake and jug of water appeared. He slept again, but was awakened by the Angel to eat. Then he walked forty days and nights to Mount Horeb. Violent storms, followed by a gentle breeze, announced God's presence. God asked why he was there. Elijah told of the rejection of the covenant and desecration of His altars. He was ordered to the Damascus desert. After anointing Hazael of Syria and Jehu of Israel, he would meet Elisha the prophet, his successor.

# ELISHA WATCHES ELIJAH TAKEN TO HEAVEN

*2 Kings 2:1-22*

SINCE Elisha was to be Elijah's successor, he wanted to spend as much time with Elijah as possible to learn about the role and lifestyle of a prophet. Elisha was also aware that he and Elijah would not have much time together, feeling that God would take Elijah in a short while.

As Elijah journeyed, Elisha made it clear he wanted to follow Elijah. This was not according to Elijah's wishes. "Stay here," Elijah had said. But Elisha replied, "As the Lord lives, and as you yourself live, I will not leave you." In Bethel they were greeted by many other prophets who asked Elisha, "Do you not know the Lord will take your master from you today?"

This time Elijah asked Elisha to remain in Bethel, but he would not hear of it. They went on to Jericho in company with numerous other prophets. The issue of Elisha's departure was again raised by the others. Elisha said he was aware of the leave-taking, and asked them: "Be still!" By the time they reached the Jordan, fifty prophets were with them. Elijah took his mantle and rolled it up and struck the river that divided so the two could cross on dry land. Elijah's cloak was a sign of God's power. It also recalled the parting of the Red Sea. All this was not lost on Elisha.

Once they were across the Jordan, God made His presence known to them. Elijah asked Elisha whether or not there was anything he could do for him. It was clear Elijah's departure time had come. Elisha asked to receive a double portion of Elijah's spirit. However this would be a difficult gift for Elijah to confer. He said, "If you wish to see me taken up from you, your wish will be granted; otherwise it will not." As they walked along talking, a flaming chariot with two flaming horses came between them. Elijah was taken up to heaven in a whirlwind riding the flaming chariot.

When Elisha could no longer see the chariot, he tore his cloak in two. He then took Elijah's cloak to the Jordan, striking the water. He cried out, "Where is the Lord, the God of Elijah?" The water parted and he crossed over. There he met the prophets who had remained behind. Those now became his followers. The power of God that Elijah had was now Elisha's.

# KING JOSIAH

### 2 Kings 22:1—23:28

JOSIAH mounted the throne when he was eight years old and governed for thirty-one years. Both his father and his grandfather had turned away from the Lord. The people had conspired against Amon his father, and he was killed. Like his ancestor David, Josiah was pleasing to the Lord and observed His laws strictly.

After eighteen years as king, Josiah decided to renovate the temple. In the process he had Shaphan, a member of a leading family and his secretary, go to the high priest Hilkiah. He wanted all the precious metals that had been donated to the temple to be melted down. They were to be given to the construction supervisors who, in turn, would use them to pay the workers making temple repairs.

At the same time, Hilkiah told Shaphan he found the book of the law in the temple. Shaphan read it, and reported to the king his errand was complete. He told Josiah of the book and read it aloud to the king. Hearing the words in the book, the king thought back to the actions of his ancestors. He became fearful for Judah's future as he realized his forebearers' actions against the Lord merited His punishment.

Josiah wanted a second opinion about the book's effect on Judah and sent it to the prophetess Hulda. Her reaction was troubling. She believed Judah would be punished for its long chronicle of sinfulness. However, since the king was sincerely disturbed over the consequences, Judah would, in her view, not be punished until after Josiah's death.

Quickly, Josiah called together all the priests, prophets and people, both high and low. He had the contents of the book read aloud. Then he made a covenant with God that all Judah would follow Him and observe His laws. He also told the high priest Hilkiah to remove all objects honoring Baal and other lesser gods. All these materials were burned outside the city of Jerusalem. Priests appointed by former kings and judges who had participated in ceremonies for Baal or other gods were banished from the temple.

Finally, Josiah directed that the Passover of the Lord be observed by all the people. This had not been done during the time of the judges and other kings. It reestablished the foundation of God's people.

# KING NEBUCHADNEZZAR OF BABYLON

*2 Kings 23:29—25:7*

DESPITE King Josiah's attempts to bring his people back to full observance of the law of Moses, God's anger at Judah was abiding. The Lord said, "Even Judah I will remove from My sight as I did Israel. I will reject Jerusalem." In Josiah's end times, Pharaoh Neco moved toward the Euphrates River, and Josiah confronted him and was killed.

Josiah's son Jehoahaz, made king by the people, was captured and died three months later. Another son, Eliakim, was appointed king by Pharaoh Neco, who changed his name to Jehoiakim. He reigned for eleven years in Jerusalem. Of an evil inclination, he did not please the Lord.

Meanwhile, Nebuchadnezzar had become king of Babylon. He moved against Jehoiakim, and he defeated him and made him his vassal for three years. Suddenly, Jehoiakim rebelled against the Babylonian king. In His anger, the Lord allowed bands of Arameans, Moabites and Ammonites to attack Judah and destroy it. Jehoiachin succeeded Jehoiakim. He too sinned in the sight of the Lord.

In his time Nebuchadnezzar attacked Jerusalem, putting the city under siege. At this, Jehoiachin, his aides, ministers and mother surrendered to Nebuchadnezzar. Then Nebuchadnezzar confiscated all the temple treasures, as well as those of the king's palace. The golden vessels dating back to Solomon's time were broken up and melted down. Ten thousand officers and men were deported. All craftsmen and metalsmiths were also sent away. Everyone was forced to go to Babylon, where they would remain as slaves for the remainder of their days. Only the poor remained in Jerusalem and had to take care of themselves.

In place of Jehoiachin, the king appointed his uncle Mattania king. His name was changed to Zedekiah. Zedekiah also did evil in God's sight, taking all his orders from Babylon. Judah was defeated in a bitter and humiliating way. Totally beaten and having access only to resources allowed by Babylon, Zedekiah was forced to rebel against Babylon. Too weak to mount a real rebellion, he was captured and blinded. His two sons were slain. The destruction of Jerusalem and Judah was complete.

# THE PROPHET ISAIAH

*Isaiah 6:1—7:15*

FROM time to time, Israel and Judah would experience challenges from other nations as well as periods of internal unrest. Yet, God always provided a great leader or prophet to bring His people back to their faith in God. A prophet from Judah, named Isaiah, would play a significant role in helping Israel and Judah rebuild their relation with God.

One day while Isaiah was praying in the temple, he was granted the great privilege of seeing God's throne in a vision. "I saw the Lord seated high on a lofty throne, and the train of His robe filled the temple." He saw Angels hovering around the throne and was aware of a great choir singing, "Holy, holy, holy is the Lord of hosts. The whole earth is full of His glory." The voices caused the temple doorframe to shake and the building was filled with smoke, a symbolic reminder of the clouds that surrounded God at Mount Sinai.

Isaiah was filled with fear. Then an Angel came to him with a burning ember taken from the altar. He touched the ember to Isaiah's lips, thus symbolically purified so as to be worthy of his vocation as God's prophet. Isaiah then heard the voice of the Lord say, "Whom shall I send?" At this, Isaiah told the Lord he was ready and willing to be sent.

Then Isaiah spoke to his king. It was a difficult and dangerous time with threats from both Syria and Israel planning to attack Jerusalem. Isaiah's king wanted to ask Syria for help. But the prophet counseled against this. As bad as the situation had become, Isaiah felt the king would do better trusting in God. If the king would ask for a sign from God, Jerusalem would be spared from all her enemies. The king preferred to put his trust in a pagan king, a sure sign that the nation would refuse to turn to God. As the king's obstinacy grew stronger, Isaiah attempted even more to have the king turn back to the Lord.

Still, Isaiah told the king God would send a sign, even though unwanted. There would be a Child born of a virgin, called Immanuel, meaning "with us is God." Immanuel's peace would fill the entire world. There would be peace between God and His people. In the future days of distress for Judah, peace would be preserved. This Immanuel would be an ideal king.

# JEREMIAH THE PROPHET

*Jeremiah 37:1—38:12*

JEREMIAH was born in a small village near Jerusalem. From an early age, he was interested in the politics of his day, and favored his king's reforms. After King Josiah's death, the people again began to stray from the word of the Lord, worship lesser gods and lead lives outside God's law. Jeremiah, called by God to be His prophet, strongly opposed the alarming return to idolatry. Due to his youth, people refused to take Jeremiah seriously. He was convinced his people were doomed and lived to witness the capture and destruction of Jerusalem.

During King Zedekiah's reign, Jeremiah urged him to stand up to those who bitterly opposed his attempts at reform. Though the king and his followers would not listen, the king said to Jeremiah, "Pray to the Lord our God for us." Following this, God spoke to Jeremiah. He was to tell Zedekiah that Pharaoh's army, which was coming to help him, would return to Egypt. God further warned that the Chaldeans would attack Jerusalem, capture and burn it. The message infuriated Zedekiah's princes and they took Jeremiah, beat him and threw him into prison at the house of Jonathan, a scribe.

Later, Zedekiah had Jeremiah brought to his palace and asked if there was a message from God. Jeremiah answered that Zedekiah would be captured by the king of Babylon. Jeremiah then asked why he was in jail. He did not want to go back to Jonathan's house for he feared the princes would kill him. So, Zedekiah ordered he be kept in the palace guard house, and he was to have one loaf of bread each day until the city's supply ran out.

Two priests told Zedekiah that Jeremiah predicted that all who remained in Jerusalem would die by the sword, famine or pestilence. Those who surrendered to the Chaldeans would be spared. The princes heard this and wanted Jeremiah put to death. The king allowed the princes to take Jeremiah. They threw him in a well without water, and the prophet sank in the muddy bottom. He was left there to starve to death.

A Cushite, Ebed-melech, told the king what the princes did to Jeremiah. The king ordered Ebed-melech to take three men and get Jeremiah out of the well, and they freed him with the aid of ropes and rags taken from the palace.

# THE BABYLONIAN EXILE

*Jeremiah 52:1-28*

KING Zedekiah supported evil in his kingdom despite God's warnings. Having sworn fealty to King Nebuchadnezzar of Babylon, he also became proud and self-assertive and rebelled against Babylon. The princes, priests and people of Judah were involved in all kinds of sinful activities, including desecrating the Lord's temple in Jerusalem.

Time after time God sent messengers to the people of Judah. He told of His love for them, but scolded them for their sinful actions. The people did not listen to God's messengers; they mistreated them. God became so angry with the people of Judah that nothing prevented His sending them punishments.

The king of the Chaldeans was sent against the leaders and people of Judah. People were slain in their own worship places. In addition, all the utensils of God's house, the treasures of the Lord, as well as those of the king and his princes were stolen and taken to Babylon.

The temple was burned and the walls of Jerusalem demolished. Palaces were set on fire and completely destroyed. About seven thousand survivors were captured and marched in disgrace to Babylon. They became unpaid servants and serfs to the king of Babylon, his sons and government officials. They would remain in virtual slavery for nearly twenty-seven years.

In the middle of all the confusion surrounding the fall of Jerusalem, King Zedekiah attempted to make his escape. He took the Jericho road toward the Jordan River. He never made it to Jericho, having been captured in the desert near Jericho.

At the time, Nebuchadnezzar's headquarters were at Ribalah in Syria. Zedekiah was taken there and condemned by the king. He watched as his three sons were put to the sword before his eyes were gouged out.

All the people who had been taken into exile in Babylon suffered much. Moreover, they were despised servants in a foreign land. With little hope of release, they felt God would never forgive them for turning away from Him. Later, as they admitted their sinfulness as a people, prayer was difficult. Many wished to turn back to God. It was for them a question whether or not God would listen.

# BELSHAZZAR'S BANQUET

*Daniel 5:1-13*

KING Nebuchadnezzar's kingdom was taken from him by the Lord who was upset with his boastful pride. Babylon then came under control of the king's son Belshazzar, who was given to much drinking and feasting. Once he invited a thousand high-ranking Babylon men and their wives to a banquet.

After a while, as the celebration grew long and Belshazzar consumed much drink, he ordered the gold and silver chalices that his father had taken from the Jerusalem temple to be brought into the banquet hall. Then the king, his lords, their wives and the entertainers drank wine from the goblets. At the same time, all the people joined in praise of their false gods. This was both a terrible desecration and a blasphemy.

As the king toasted the Babylonian gods, the pagan rituals were suddenly interrupted. Opposite the king's lampstand, a large figure of a human hand appeared and began to write on the plaster wall. Belshazzar was struck with fear.

The king shouted for the enchanters and astrologers to be assembled immediately. He pledged, "Whoever reads this writing and interprets its meaning shall be clothed in purple, wear a chain of gold about his neck and rank third in the government of the kingdom." But no one could interpret the writing. When his queen was advised of the king's condition, she came to the banquet hall to calm and assure him all would be well.

"O king, live forever! Do not be troubled in mind, or let your face grow pale. In your kingdom there is a man in whom is the spirit of the holy God." She went on to explain that during Belshazzar's father's reign this individual was discovered and believed to have tremendous knowledge "and wisdom like the gods." She told how the king's father had appointed the man chief of the magicians, enchanters and astrologers because of his extraordinary mind.

That man's Jewish name was Daniel This man knew how to understand and interpret dreams. He was a great problem solver. "Now call Daniel to tell you what this means." The king responded immediately to the queen's suggestion even though following her directions was a great humiliation for him.

# DANIEL AND THE WRITING ON THE WALL

*Daniel 5:13—6:1*

KING Belshazzar was recovering from the shock of the appearance of a human handwriting on the wall, when Daniel was brought before him. He said, "Are you Daniel, an exile of Judah, whom my father the king brought from Judah?" Belshazzar told Daniel he had heard people say he was possessed of the spirit of God, along with great knowledge and wisdom. He retold how he summoned his wise men and enchanters to read the message on the wall, but they were unable to do so. Further, he stated he had heard Daniel could interpret the writing as well as dreams. If that proved to be true, Daniel would be greatly respected and have high ranking in the kingdom's government.

Daniel told the king he was not interested in the offered gifts, and, bordering on insolence, told the king he could give the gifts to someone else. "But I will read for you the writing, O king, and tell you its meaning." Then, almost as if giving a history lesson, Daniel reminded Belshazzar how his father Nebuchadnezzar had been given a great kingdom with glorious majesty. But his pride and insolence grew so much that God took away the throne and his glory vanished. He ended his life with wild asses and ate the grass like an ox. He stayed in those degrading conditions until he learned a very important lesson, which was "that the Most High God rules over the kingdom of mortals and sets over it whom He will."

Addressing Belshazzar as "his son," Daniel reminded the king that he had not humbled himself before God. In a boastful way, the king had the temple vessels brought into the banquet hall so his courtiers, their wives and friends could drink wine from them. He reminded the king further how he had taken the lead in praising and honoring the false gods of silver, gold, bronze, iron wood and stone "that do not see or hear or have intelligence." Finally, Daniel scolded the king also for not glorifying God during his life. It was the same God Who sent the wrist and hand to write on the wall.

Daniel then told Belshazzar what the writing meant. God had numbered the days of his kingdom and put an end to it. The king had been evaluated in God's eyes and was found unfit as king. And Belshazzar's kingdom was divided in two between the Medes and Persians. Calmly, despite the devastating information, the king ordered Daniel clothed with the items of his new office. Later that night Belshazzar was slain and Darius the Mede took over the kingdom.

# DANIEL IN THE LIONS' DEN

*Daniel 6:2-27*

WHEN King Darius ascended his throne, he appointed one hundred twenty subordinates to look after his interests throughout the kingdom. They reported to three supervisors, of which Daniel was one. In a short time, Daniel pleased the king with his leadership ability. The king decided to give Daniel charge of his supervisors. Of course, the other supervisors and subordinates resented Daniel and looked for a way to bring him down.

The only way to trap Daniel was through a violation of the law. Several of Daniel's opponents went to the king and successfully convinced him there should be a decree prohibiting anyone from addressing a petition to any god or man except the king over a thirty-day period. The king agreed and issued an "unchanging and irrevocable" decree to that effect under law.

Daniel continued his daily routine of praying at home to God three times a day. He always kept the windows facing Jerusalem open in his prayer chamber. One day, several opponents rushed into Daniel's home and caught him praying to his God. They went to the king, reminding Darius of the decree. Although Darius wanted to save Daniel, he could not. Darius admitted the decree was absolute and irrevocable.

Searching for a decision, the king delayed until sundown. Then he ordered Daniel brought before him and sentenced his top supervisor to be cast into the lions' den, saying, "May your God, whom you serve so faithfully, save you." Then Daniel was put into the deep pit. It was impossible to climb its walls, and its entrance was sealed with a large stone. Returning to his palace, Darius refused to eat and spent a sleepless night.

Early the next day Darius went to the den and called out, asking Daniel if he was all right. Daniel answered, "O king, live forever. My God has sent His Angel and shut the lions' mouths so they would not hurt me." Those who accused Daniel along with their wives and children were put into the den and they were caught and crushed by the lions. Then King Darius wrote to all nations and peoples, "Peace to you. I decree that in every dominion in my kingdom, the God of Daniel is to be reverenced and feared."

# RETURN TO JERUSALEM

*Ezra 1:1—3:13*

IN the first year of the reign of Cyrus, king of Persia, the word of God announced by the prophet Jeremiah was fulfilled. Cyrus issued a proclamation to all the earthly kingdoms that God had given him. He said that God had ordered him to build the Lord's house in Jerusalem in Judah. Any people throughout Cyrus' kingdoms who belonged to God's people were free to go up to Jerusalem. Their servitude in Babylon had come to an end.

It was the dawn of a new age for God's people, a gift and fulfillment of the promise that exile would eventually come to an end. Wherever they might have lived during the time of exile, the people of those regions were to assist the Israelites with "silver, gold, goods, cattle and freewill offerings" for God's house in Jerusalem. Those who decided to return would share in the donations.

God inspired many heads of families of the houses of Judah and Benjamin, along with priests and Levites, to return to Jerusalem. Great preparations went on for the return journey. This time the people would migrate with relatively few challenges and disputes. Neighbors gave as much help as they could manage. The utensils and sacred vessels taken by Nebuchadnezzar were given by King Cyrus to Sheshbazzar, a prince of Judah, who was to take them back to Jerusalem for use in the new temple.

Once the Jewish people arrived in Jerusalem, their worst fears were confirmed. All was in ruins, and before the people could turn to rebuilding the temple, they had to build homes and cultivate farmlands for food. A long time passed and attempts were made to rebuild the temple. Still, around seven months after the Israelites settled at Jerusalem, under the leadership of Jeshua, the priests and people built an altar of the God of Israel on which, in accordance with the law of Moses, they could offer holocausts to the Lord morning and evening.

Despite fears of some remaining local peoples, holocausts were offered as prescribed at the new moons and other festivals. Still, the temple foundation had not yet been started.

In preparation for building the temple, stone cutters and carpenters were hired. Oil and food were traded with the Sidonians and Tyrians for large cedar trees.

Levites over twenty years old were appointed supervisors. Once the foundations were laid, vested priests praised the Lord with songs of thanksgiving saying, "for He is good, for His mercy toward Israel endures forever." Many who remembered the former temple cried out in sorrow, while others danced for joy.

# JONAH AND THE WHALE

*Jonah 1:2—3:11*

AS God's favored people, the Israelites tended to feel the Lord had a very narrow view of nonbelievers. This thinking sometimes reached the minds and hearts of some of God's prophets. Jonah was one of these.

God called upon Jonah to bring His message to the people in the city of Nineveh. Although Jonah had a very narrow and prejudiced opinion of the Ninevites, his mission was to preach within the city in an attempt to bring its people to acknowledge the truth of God's word. Instead of accepting his assignment in humble obedience, Jonah decided to escape to Tarshish. The Hebrews considered it one of the most remote western places, a perfect area for Jonah to hide from the Lord.

Jonah took a boat from Joppa. Soon, a wild storm threatened to sink the ship. It was God's punishment for Jonah's disobedience. Since the sailors came to know this through prayer for safety, they asked God not to charge them with murder if they threw Jonah overboard. A whale swallowed Jonah when he was thrown overboard. Safe in the whale's belly for three days and nights, Jonah prayed to the Lord.

"But with resounding praise I will sacrifice to you; I will pay what I have vowed: salvation is from the Lord." After three days and nights, the whale spit Jonah upon the shore.

Jonah then made his way to Nineveh. Upon his arrival there, to Jonah's great surprise, the Ninevites listened to the Lord's message of approaching doom and responded positively. All from the king to his lowliest subjects humbled themselves in sackcloth and ashes. The king further ordered that both men and animals were not to eat food or drink water. All were to turn from their evil ways, especially violence. The king hoped God would pull back from His threat to destroy the city. When God saw the Ninevites' spirit of repentance, He withdrew His threat.

Jonah was not pleased with God's forgiveness. He felt the Ninevites got off easy. Like many fellow Israelites, Jonah was wide open to the mercy of God for Israel but not for pagan nations. Jonah's role as prophet demonstrates that many threats God sent to peoples and nations were but the expression of God's merciful will calling all to seek forgiveness.

# Bridging the Testaments

BEFORE moving on to the New Testament, it is important to pause and consider the great bridge of the Old and New Testaments: the Psalms, or Psalter.

Some may wonder why the Church makes use of Psalms from ancient times in order to pray in our day. Isn't she capable of creating new prayers? In truth, the creativity of the Church is evidenced in many other ways. However, she knows that there is no need for new Psalms since these were the work of the Holy Spirit. They are *inspired prayers,* appropriate for all times.

The Church knows and teaches that there is only one economy of salvation and it includes both the Old and the New Covenant. The Psalter is *the* prayer book for this entire history—containing both thanksgiving for the wonders that God has already accomplished and expectation for the promises of the Kingdom.

Let us join in thanking God for all He has done and continues to do for us by praying from Psalm 100:

> Acclaim the LORD with joy, all the earth;
>     serve the LORD with gladness;
>     enter his presence with songs of joy.
>
> Proclaim that the LORD is God.
>     He made us and we are his possession;
>     we are his people, the flock he shepherds.
>
> Offer thanksgiving as you enter his gates,
>     sing hymns of praise as you approach
>         his courts;
> give thanks to him and bless his name,
>     for the LORD is good.
> His kindness endures forever,
>     and his faithfulness is constant to all
>         generations.

# Introduction to the New Testament

AS we move into the New Testament, we soon realize there is a major connection between the two divisions of the Bible. We really cannot go forward with the words God has given us until we understand all that was written and spoken concerning God over four thousand years before the time of Christ.

As the story of God's people continues in the New Testament, we are not unaware of the great events of the creation of the universe; Adam and Eve's fall from grace and expulsion from Eden; the rise of Moses, the reformer sent by the Lord to bring back from slavery His people, who turned away from and returned to God.

Underlying all these ups and downs was the hope for a Messiah, One Who would bring back the Lord's people to a sense of responsibility to God and for one another. The New Testament turns out to be a breathtaking account of the Messiah's coming to earth, His life on earth, and His call to repentance and everlasting life.

Jesus, our God and Savior, came that we might have a more abundant and joy-filled life, a contrast to a life of sensual self-indulgence and sin. His stories are in the Gospels of Matthew, Mark, Luke and John, and a variety of other writers. Like the prophets' words, their writings and preaching were guided by the Holy Spirit. Unlike the prophets of old, the Gospel writers and others lived close to or at the time of Jesus.

Still, the messages of the evangelists and prophets were much the same. Jesus preached the idea of turning away from sin and back to God with contrite hearts. He spoke often of God's spirit of forgiveness. God showed the depth of His love in the death and resurrection of Jesus. Furthermore, He sent the Holy Spirit to remain with us until the end of time.

# ZECHARIAH AND ELIZABETH

*Luke 1:5-25*

WHEN Herod was king of Judea, Zechariah and his wife Elizabeth were known to be God-fearing people. They lived strictly according to God's law. Zechariah, a priest, was faithful to his religious duties. Unfortunately, Elizabeth was unable to bear children. As old age approached, despite all their prayers, they began to lose hope of ever having a child.

One time, Zechariah had been elected by his brother priests to burn incense in the temple. While he was doing so, the community remained in prayer outside. Suddenly, an Angel appeared. He became frightened, but the Angel comforted him, saying, "Do not be afraid, Zechariah, because your prayer has been heard. Your wife will bear a son, and you shall name him John."

Then the Angel told Zechariah that many people would be happy over John's birth, and that this son would be filled with the Holy Spirit, "even from his mother's womb." John was to lead his people back to the Lord and prepare them for the Messiah.

Greatly surprised by the news, Zechariah asked how this would come about since he and his wife were elderly. Then Zechariah asked the Angel who he was. It was the Angel Gabriel. Since Zechariah did not believe the Angel's message right away, he would remain speechless until John's birth.

Those watching outside the temple wondered why Zechariah stayed so long. When he came out he was unable to speak. They took that as a sign he had seen a vision.

Elizabeth soon conceived and went into seclusion. In Judaism, Elizabeth's childlessness was looked upon as a punishment for sin. Despite the shame and talk, Elizabeth and Zechariah remained steadfast in their faith.

When Elizabeth gave birth, friends and neighbors gathered in great joy. After eight days, the child was circumcised and given a name. Many expected he would be named after his father. But Elizabeth said the name was John. Some said she had no relatives of that name. They asked Zechariah about the name. He wrote, "His name is John." At that moment Zechariah's speech returned and many were filled with fear.

# THE ANNUNCIATION

*Luke 1:26-38*

THE Angel Gabriel was sent to the small town of Nazareth located in the poverty-ridden province of Galilee. A poor virgin named Mary lived there. She was engaged to a self-employed carpenter named Joseph, who belonged to the house of David.

Gabriel surprised Mary with his arrival and proclaimed, "Hail, favored one! The Lord is with you." These words upset Mary since she did not understand their meaning. Going on, Gabriel told Mary not to be afraid, because God looked upon her with great favor. As a result, Mary would conceive a Child, a Son, and was to call Him Jesus. "He will be great and will be called Son of the Most High, and He will rule over the house of Jacob forever and of His kingdom there will be no end."

Mary was both surprised and frightened by the Angel's message. She protested that she was engaged, but not yet married. Gabriel explained that the Holy Spirit would come to her and the power of God would surround her. The Child to be born was to be proclaimed holy and called the Son of God.

At the same time, the Angel told Mary that her cousin Elizabeth in her old age was also with child. She too would give birth to a son. Finally, Mary was reminded that with God everything is possible. Mary replied, "Behold the handmaid of the Lord. May it be done to me according to your word." After Mary's reply, the Angel left. As the Church teaches us today, Mary's yes to the will of God meant that all peoples of every era could share in the life of the Father.

While Mary was listening to Gabriel and trying to absorb his message, a number of emotions stirred in the young girl. But she wondered about God's miracles with which she would be involved. The realization that God asked her to carry out His special mission made her physically weak, but also uplifted. As her fear began to gradually disappear and calm and quiet returned to her humble home, Mary's thoughts turned to Joseph, her fiancé. How would he react? What would she say to him to explain all the coming events that would affect their shared lives?

# THE VISITATION

*Luke 1:39-56*

WHEN Mary told Joseph about the Angel's visit, he was both confused and wary. He realized Mary was pregnant outside marriage and would be treated harshly. The law required that if a woman became pregnant outside marriage, she was to be publicly stoned to death. Joseph did not want to have Mary punished so he decided to break their engagement.

That night an Angel appeared to Joseph in a dream. He told Joseph not to be afraid to have Mary as his wife, since her Child was conceived through the power of the Holy Spirit. Also, the Son to be born of her would bring hope and salvation to God's people. Hearing this, Joseph took Mary into his home.

Amid such upheaval, Mary remembered her cousin Elizabeth was also pregnant and probably in need of help. She set out into the hill country and went to Zechariah's home in Judah. When Mary entered Zechariah's home, she called out to Elizabeth. When Elizabeth heard Mary's voice, the infant leaped in her womb. Elizabeth, then filled with the Holy Spirit, cried out in a loud voice, "Most blessed are you among women, and blessed is the fruit of your womb. And who am I that the mother of my Lord should come to me? For the moment the sound of your greeting reached my ears, the infant in my womb leaped for joy."

The words "who am I" recall the words of King David when the Ark of the Covenant was taken back to Jerusalem after its capture by the Philistines. There is a tight connection between the Old Testament and New Testament in the visit of Mary to Elizabeth. David and his people strongly believed the Ark symbolized God's presence. When Mary visited Zechariah's house to help her cousin, the home was made holy through the divine presence of the Lord in Mary's womb.

Mary replied to Elizabeth with a variety of Old Testament quotes reflecting the Messiah. Mary's words told of God's desire to open His kingdom to all people. Salvation was to be for all—not just for the higher classes, as was thought before the coming of Christ, but also for the lowly. Mary stayed three months until Elizabeth gave birth.

# THE BIRTH OF JESUS

*Luke 2:1-20*

AFTER Mary returned home from Zechariah's house to await the birth of her Child, she and Joseph made the usual plans to receive a child into the home. When it was nearly time for Mary to give birth, Caesar Augustus, emperor of the Roman Empire, required the whole world to be registered. All were to go to their hometowns. This meant that Joseph and Mary had to go from Nazareth in the province of Galilee to Bethlehem, a town of the house of David, in Judea. Because Joseph was of David's clan, he and Mary had to enroll there.

When they arrived in Bethlehem, Mary was about to give birth. Due to the registration, the town was crowded. It was difficult to find shelter, and Mary and Joseph could not afford some places. But they did find cover in an innkeeper's barn. There Mary gave birth to Jesus. The Baby was wrapped in swaddling clothes, the same kind of dress that was given Solomon, David's son, at his birth. The Baby was put to bed in a manger, a feeding trough for the animals.

At the same time, shepherds who were tending their flocks in the region were surprised and frightened by the appearance of an Angel. The Angel said to the shepherds, "Do not be afraid, for I bring you good news of great joy for all the people. For this day, in the city of David, there has been born to you a Savior Who is Christ, the Lord."

Once the Angel completed his message, a large choir of heavenly spirits appeared with the Angel praising God and singing, "Glory to God in the highest, and on earth peace to those on whom his favor rests."

The shepherds were stunned and bewildered until after the Angel and his choir left. Recovered, they said to each other, "Come, let us go then, to Bethlehem to see this thing that has taken place, which the Lord has made known to us." They went quickly to the innkeeper's barn. They were the first to arrive on the scene. And they shared the Angel's message with those who were in the area. The ones who heard the shepherd's story were amazed. The shepherds arrival, adoration, conduct and departure left Joseph and Mary considering all that had happened that night.

# THE PRESENTATION

*Luke 2:21-40*

EIGHT days after the birth of Jesus, according to Mosaic law, Joseph and Mary arranged to have Jesus circumcised. At that time, their Child's name became official and He was registered in His hometown. Here, too, they followed the Angel's direction concerning Jesus' name.

According to Mosaic law also, a woman who gave birth to a boy is unable for forty days to touch anything sacred or to enter the temple area because of her legal impurity. At the end of forty days, she is required to offer a year-old lamb as a burnt offering and a turtle dove or young pigeon to expel sin. If she could not afford a lamb, two turtle doves or two young pigeons would do.

So, forty days after Jesus' birth, Mary and Joseph took Him to the temple for both Mary's purification and Jesus' presentation. According to the law of the Lord, every firstborn male was to be consecrated to the Lord. Since Joseph and Mary lived in poverty, two turtle doves were offered.

Meanwhile, a holy and blessed man, Simeon, prayed to be allowed to live to see the birth of the Messiah. He learned through the Holy Spirit that he would not die before the Messiah came.

Moved by the Spirit, he went to the temple the very day Mary and Joseph brought Jesus there for His consecration. When Simeon saw them, he was overwhelmed with joy.

Mary and Joseph allowed him to hold Jesus. He praised the Lord and proclaimed, "Now, Lord, You may dismiss Your servant in peace, according to Your word; for my eyes have seen Your salvation, which You have prepared in sight of all the peoples, a light of revelation to the Gentiles and glory for Your people Israel." Mary and Joseph were shocked by his words.

Then Simeon blessed Mary and Joseph. He spoke to Mary about how Jesus was destined to be fully involved in the fall and rise of many in Israel. He would call God's people to follow and listen. Some would not accept Him. Others would take His words to heart.

In her Son's lifetime, Mary would have her heart broken. Her Son's enemies would inflict physical and verbal abuse on Him. Some would plot His death. In the temple an elderly prophetess, Anna, came forward praising God for Jesus' birth. Mary and Joseph returned to Nazareth and nurtured Jesus.

# THE FLIGHT INTO EGYPT

*Matthew 2:13-23*

AFTER the birth of Jesus, astrologers from the East, having noticed a new star that appeared in the sky, thought the time of a new King had come according to their traditions. They set out to locate the King near the star. Upon their arrival in Jerusalem, the star disappeared. Since they were of the princely class, they asked King Herod about the star and the newborn King.

Herod was upset at the news of a newborn King. He sought information from his advisors and asked where, according to their knowledge, the Messiah was to be born. They told of the prophet's note that the birth would take place in Bethlehem: "And you, Bethlehem, in the land of Judah, are by no means least among the rulers of Judah, for from you shall come a Ruler Who will shepherd My people Israel."

In a secret meeting, Herod asked the Easterners when the star appeared and advised them to go to Bethlehem and search for the Child. Then they were to give His location to Herod on their return trip. Once they left Jerusalem, the star reappeared and stopped where Mary, Joseph and the Child were. Presenting their gifts and homage, the men rested before leaving for home. An Angel warned them in a dream not to go back to Herod, so they traveled a different route.

Once the visitors left Bethlehem, an Angel of the Lord appeared to Joseph and told him, "Arise, take the Child and His Mother, and flee to Egypt. Remain there until I tell you. Herod seeks the Child to kill Him." Herod became very angry when he realized the Easterners went home an alternate way. He realized that someone must have alerted the new King's parents, and they fled. In a vain attempt to cast a net to catch them, Herod ordered all males in Bethlehem and its vicinity, two years old and under, to be put to death.

For Mary, Joseph and the Child the trip to Egypt was a difficult one. They had to flee in a hurry across hill country and into desert plains that could be dangerous and inhospitable. Why did the Angel send them on such a challenging journey? Egypt was a traditional place of refuge for those fleeing Palestine. It was almost as if Mary, Joseph and Jesus were about to relive the Exodus of the Israelites of old.

After the death of Herod, Joseph was told in a dream,

"Arise, take the Child and His Mother, and go to the land of Israel, for those who sought to kill the Child are dead." Since Herod's sons were not open to the new King, the family was warned not to go to Bethlehem, and they settled in Galilee, in the town of Nazareth.

# JESUS IS FOUND IN THE TEMPLE

*Luke 2:41-52*

WHEN Jesus was taken back to Nazareth, He lived with His parents and grew up in their home. His father was a carpenter, while His mother cared for their home. Their town was small, and the area was poor, so life for them was a daily struggle. Mary and Joseph were good Jewish people and observed the Mosaic law to the best of their ability. Each year they would go on pilgrimage to Jerusalem to celebrate the rites of Passover.

When Jesus was twelve years old, they went up to Jerusalem as usual. Following the celebrations they returned to Nazareth, but did not know that Jesus remained in Jerusalem. Mary and Joseph, according to custom, traveled separately, Mary with the women and Joseph with the men. Each thought Jesus was with the other. At the end of the first day on the road, Mary and Joseph checked with their relatives and friends to see if Jesus was with them. But He was nowhere to be found.

With heavy and anxious hearts, the two went back to Jerusalem and looked for Jesus over three days. Finally, they found Him in the temple area. They were really surprised to find Jesus among a group of temple teachers of the law. He was listening to them and also asking questions. Others were watching their give and take. The teachers were amazed at his poise and wisdom. The teachers too were surprised at Jesus' questions, which demonstrated a great depth of knowledge.

Of course, Mary and Joseph were totally taken off guard by what they saw. But their surprise was soon overcome with disappointment and hurt to think that Jesus would have stayed behind without telling them. Mary asked Jesus why He did this to them, explaining He had caused them much anxiety. Jesus' answer sounded almost disrespectful. "Why were you searching for Me? Did you not know that I must be in My Father's house?" Yet, obediently, Jesus gathered His belongings and set out with His parents for home.

When they arrived home, it was as if nothing happened. Jesus remained obedient to his parents. Still, Mary kept thinking of what He had said to them in the temple. She was troubled over the meaning of Jesus' words and what they could portend for their future.

# THE BAPTISM OF JESUS

*Matthew 3:13-17*

JESUS remained at home in Nazareth till He was about thirty years old. In the meantime, Elizabeth's son, John the Baptist, had also grown to adulthood. While John was actively seeking God's will, the Lord came to John in the desert. It was a call to preach the word of God. He is sometimes considered to have been a prophet, since his call to minister to God's people was similar to that of the prophets. In some instances, John was described as "more than a prophet." Frequently, he is understood as a bridge between the Old Testament prophets and the fulfillment of the prophecy and promise of a Messiah.

As Jesus began His public life of preaching the good news of salvation, He first went to the area of the Jordan River in order to seek baptism from John the Baptist. John had been there preaching the message of repentance. Sometimes John in his preaching called his listeners "a brood of vipers," who needed to demonstrate their sorrow for sin. He warned of those whose lives did not produce goodness and virtue.

When people asked what they should do, John stated they should share their clothing and food with the poor. He warned soldiers not to indulge in extortion or give false testimony. When people asked John if he were the Messiah, he said his baptism was of water. But the Messiah's baptism would bring the Holy Spirit and fire. In that time the people understood fire to be a refining and purifying process.

One day, Jesus came to John and asked to be baptized. At this meeting, those present watched in wonder. Realizing Jesus was closer to God than he, John felt it only fitting that Jesus should baptize him. Still, Jesus insisted with John that this was His wish and that of the Father, and both were duty bound to do God's will. John accepted this and Jesus stepped into the river.

When John poured water over Jesus, the skies parted, and the Holy Spirit in the form of a dove descended upon Jesus. And then a voice came out of the heavens, "You are My beloved Son; with You I am well pleased."

Shortly after John and Jesus parted, Herod, whom John had scolded for marrying his brother's wife, seized John and put him in prison.

# JESUS IS TEMPTED

*Matthew 4:1-11*

FOLLOWING His baptism in the Jordan River, and having bid farewell to John the Baptist, Jesus sought solitude in the desert. Inspired by the Spirit at His baptism, Jesus wanted to be alone for prayer and fasting. It was a true preparation time for His public ministry. So, for forty days and forty nights Jesus fasted and prayed in the desert. This time prepared Him to meet the most difficult challenges that lay ahead.

While still in the desert, Satan came to Jesus under the guise of a friend who wanted to help. Knowing Jesus had been fasting, Satan tempted Him to turn stones into bread. Not only did he want Jesus to break His fast, but he hoped Jesus would indulge Himself in instant gratification. Jesus answered Satan's challenge by saying, "It is written, 'One does not live on bread alone.'" Satan was stung by this answer and determined to try another trick.

Satan led Jesus to Jerusalem, had Him stand on the highest wall of the temple and said, "If you are the Son of God, throw Yourself down from here, for it is written: 'He will command His Angels concerning You, to guard You,' and 'with their hands they will support You, lest You dash Your foot against a stone.'" Of course, Jesus knew He would be protected in all circumstances, but He would not give Satan the satisfaction of throwing Himself off the wall, knowing full well He would be safe. So, Jesus said to Satan, "You shall not put the Lord your God to the test."

Still hoping for success, Satan took Jesus up to the highest mountain and pointed to all the kingdoms of the world at once, claiming, "I shall give to You all this power and their glory, for it has been handed over to me, and I may give it over to whomever I wish. All this I will give You if You worship me." Jesus knew this was a lie. So He said to Satan, "You shall worship the Lord your God, and Him alone shall you serve."

After this third rejection, Satan left Jesus. The Lord sent His Angels to care for Jesus. In all this, Jesus gave each of us a good lesson on how to deal with temptations that will inevitably come to us. Our personal Angel of the Lord will be with us to keep us away from the occasions of sin. And the Holy Spirit will guide us on how best to serve God and His will in all things.

# JESUS CALLS PETER AND ANDREW

*Luke 5:1-11*

WHEN Jesus heard that John the Baptist had been put in prison, He left Nazareth and moved on to Galilee, staying in Capernaum. One day, along the Lake of Gennesaret, many people were following Him and listening. They tried to get as close as possible in order to hear. Jesus saw two boats pulled up on the beach, and their owners were cleaning their nets after an unsuccessful night of fishing.

Jesus approached Simon Peter and asked Peter if he would take Jesus a short distance out from the shore. Peter readily agreed. When they reached a certain point out in the lake, Jesus had Peter drop anchor. Sitting down, Jesus began to preach to the people. Since His voice carried more readily over water, the people were quite happy to have Jesus talking to them from the boat.

After Jesus finished teaching the crowd, Peter began to go toward the shore. But Jesus said to Peter, "Put out into the deep and lower your nets for a catch." Peter wondered about this suggestion since he knew Jesus was not an experienced fisherman. So Peter said, "Master, we worked hard throughout the night and caught nothing, but if You say so, I will let down the nets." Peter really did not want to start fishing again. But he decided to follow Jesus' wishes.

They had not gone too far when they slipped their nets into the water. They started to haul the nets in, and the full nets were almost breaking. They signaled their partners in the other boat to help. Both boats were so full that they were afraid of the boats sinking. They returned to shore to sort the catch. That night all the fishermen were filled with fear.

Simon Peter fell on his knees before Jesus and said, "Depart from me, for I am a sinful man." But once Jesus was convinced Peter and Andrew would follow Him, He revealed the Lord's plan for the world. He said to Peter and Andrew, "Do not be afraid. From now on you will be catching men." James and John, sons of Zebedee, were so astonished at what they had seen that they too decided to go with Peter and Andrew.

# THE WEDDING FEAST AT CANA

*John 2:1-11*

WHEN Jesus returned from His desert retreat and His defeat of Satan, He received an invitation to a wedding of two friends. The celebration was held in Cana, a small town in Galilee. Mary arrived at the wedding before Jesus and His friends. The wedding feast would go on for several days, and there was much singing, dancing and feasting on food and wine. At the weddings of ordinary people, wine was very important, and it was indeed an embarrassment for any newly married couple if the wine supply was exhausted.

Mary realized this was going to happen in a short time, and she pulled Jesus aside quietly and said, "They have no wine." Jesus seemed both surprised and annoyed that Mary mentioned this. He answered, "Woman, what concern is this to us? My hour has not yet come."

This may seem a disrespectful answer. Still, Mary, in her own way, knew what to do. She told the servers, "Do whatever He tells you." In the general preparation and serving area, there were six twenty- to thirty-gallon jars for Jewish ceremonial washings. Jesus told the servers to fill the jars with water, and they filled them to the top. Then Jesus said, "Now draw some out and take it to the chief steward." They did so and the chief steward tasted the wine before serving. He was amazed at the quality and taste. He did not know where it came from, but his servers did.

The chief steward called to the bridegroom and said, "Everyone serves the choice wine first, and then an inferior vintage when the guests have been drinking for a while. You have saved the best wine until now." Jesus, in His compassion, did not want to see His newly married friends embarrassed. The celebration continued on, and most of those present were not aware of Jesus' contribution.

However, this was the beginning of Jesus' signs of His power and the mission carried out for the Father. A bit of His glory was revealed here, and, at the same time, His disciples began to believe in Him.

When they left the wedding, Jesus, His Mother and the disciples went down to Capernaum and stayed there for a few days before setting out to complete Jesus' work. He started out in Jerusalem, where His preaching and miracles began to stir the people.

# JESUS HEALS
# THE CRIPPLED MAN

*Mark 2:1-12*

AFTER Jesus went back to Capernaum, word began to get around that He was living in a house in town. Jesus felt inclined, through the inspiration of the Holy Spirit, to reach out to the ill and rejected with a variety of cures. He knew that many Pharisees and scribes, who were trained in the oral interpretation of the law, came to listen to His teachings.

At times, so many gathered in Jesus' house it was almost impossible to move. Many spilled outside while Jesus preached. One time, a group of men carried a paralyzed man to the house so he could be cured by Jesus. But, when they arrived, they saw there was no way the man could be carried through the crowd. Therefore, they opened up the roof above Jesus and lowered the crippled man. It was the faith of the paralytic and those who carried him that moved Jesus to cure the afflicted man.

When Jesus saw this great act of faith, He said to the man. "Son, your sins are forgiven." But some scribes who saw this were thinking to themselves, "How can this man say such things? He is blaspheming! Who can forgive sins but God alone?"

Jesus knew immediately what the scribes were thinking, so He said to them, "Why do you entertain such thoughts in your hearts? Which is easier to say to him, 'Your sins are forgiven,' or to say, 'Stand up, take your mat and walk' "? At that point Jesus wanted to publicly and fully demonstrate His role on earth as the "Son of Man." Further, He told them He would demonstrate His power to forgive sins. So He addressed the cripple, saying, "I say to you, stand up, take your mat and go home." The man got up, picked up the mat and made his way through the crowd and left the house.

During the confrontation between Jesus and the scribes, all eyes were fixed on them, and they heard Jesus' command to get up and leave. Astonished, they broke out in praise to God and exchanged joyful greetings, saying, "Truly we have seen wonderful things this day." Their praise joined that of the cured paralytic and convinced many to mend their ways and return to the Lord. The Pharisees and scribes were seething with anger but ignored by the crowd.

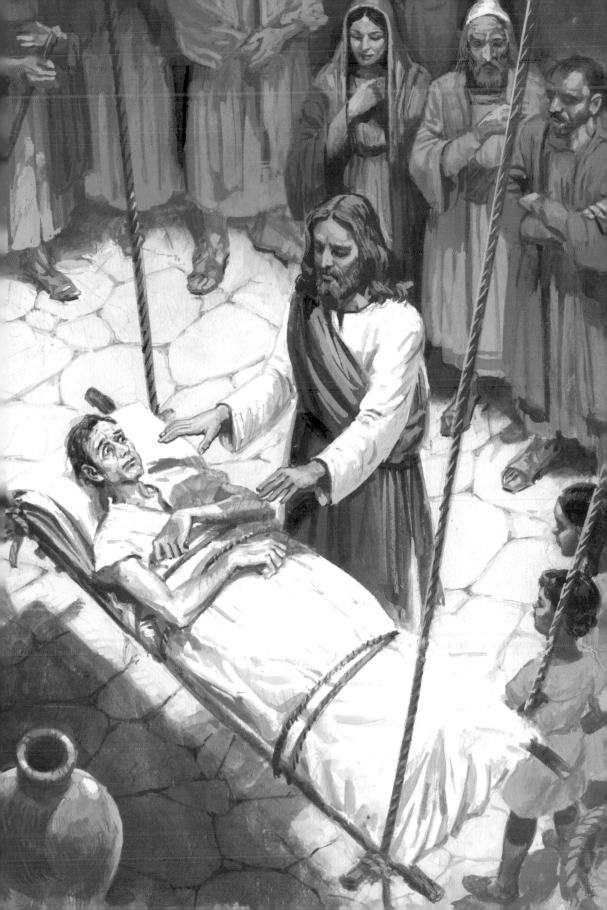

# THE SERMON ON THE MOUNT

*Matthew 5:1-12*

JESUS continued to go throughout Galilee preaching in Jewish synagogues. He constantly proclaimed the kingdom of God. At the same time, He continued to bring attention to His message by curing people of every disease and illness among the multitudes that followed Him. His fame spread. Not only were the ill brought to Him, but also the possessed, lunatics and paralytics, and He cured all.

At one time, Jesus purposefully delivered a well-organized, far-reaching discourse on a mountainside in Galilee. And a new set of directions, over and above the Ten Commandments, were presented in this special sermon. The new directions, sometimes called the Beatitudes, suggest God's people go beyond the minimums stated in the Commandments.

Jesus applauds those without material possessions, who have placed their trust in God. God will comfort the sorrowing, whether their grief comes from challenging circumstances in their lives or sorrow for personal sin. In addition, the meek would possess the land. At the same time, those who seek to carry out the will of God in their lives will be blessed and pleasing in God's eyes. Those who hunger for and seek holiness will share God's kingdom in the future and will be happy living the kingdom's values every day. In a special way, they will experience God in their lives.

Sometimes in our lives when we seek to be holy, we can easily come to the realization that we are human. At the same time, those who do not care to share the faith could become offensive with others who live their faith. When one grants mercy to a fellow human being, the world may view this as foolishness or a sign of weakness. And today we see all too clearly how those who seek to bring peace into both the world and local society are held up for ridicule and sometimes physical assault.

Our Lord told His people, "Blessed are you when people insult you and persecute you and utter all kinds of calumnies against you for My sake. Rejoice and be glad, for your reward will be great in heaven." In a very true sense, God considers all His people prophets and disciples. Therefore, a positive and virtuous lifestyle may be open to critique or attack.

# THE CENTURION

*Luke 7:1-10*

AS Jesus moved about Galilee, there were some Jewish people who could not bring themselves to a firm conviction over what Jesus was saying and doing. Sometimes many non-Jewish people could be drawn to the crowds who were listening to Jesus. Some found what He said to be a sign of hope shining through their non-religious backgrounds.

One day when Jesus was in the city of Capernaum, He was approached by friends of a centurion. The centurion was a Gentile soldier who belonged to the Roman military barracks in Capernaum. He was made aware of a wandering Prophet who had been in Capernaum for some time and had even performed amazing cures there.

The centurion sent some elders of the Jews to Jesus because he had a slave who was ill and near death. He valued his slave highly. He asked his friends to contact Jesus and ask that He might save the slave's life. The elders mentioned the situation to Jesus and urged Him to go to the ill slave, saying, "He deserves this favor from You, for he loves our people and he built our synagogue for us." So Jesus went with them. When Jesus was close to the centurion's house, he sent word with the message, "Lord, do not trouble Yourself, for I am not worthy to have You come under my roof." At that time to enter a house of a Gentile was considered unclean for a Jewish person.

The messenger explained further that he did not come to Jesus because he considered himself unworthy. He said the centurion told him how he was an individual of authority, in charge of one hundred soldiers. Further, he explained that when he gives orders, his soldiers come and go as he directs. This military man knew the power and force of a spoken command. Acknowledging Jesus as a special person, the centurion believed Jesus could cure his slave with His power without even entering his home.

When Jesus heard this He was amazed, and He turned to the crowd that followed Him, saying, "I tell you, in no one throughout Israel have I found faith as great as this." When the messenger returned to the centurion's house, he found the slave in good health.

# THE WIDOW'S SON

*Luke 7:11-17*

JESUS continued His preaching and teaching. What attracted so many people to both listen and follow Jesus was His spirit of humility and compassion. While the people of Galilee at the time of Jesus were simple, hardworking individuals, there could flare up between themselves and their Roman occupiers incidents in which compassion could easily be replaced with demeaning violence. Concerns about Jesus' activities were overcome by His nonthreatening manner.

After leaving the Capernaum area, Jesus came with the usual group of followers to the town of Naim. At the city gates, they halted out of respect for a funeral procession making its way out of town. The deceased happened to be the only son of a widow. Jesus learned this after inquiring about the identity of the deceased. When He realized the situation, Jesus, totally aware of the law and the difficult challenges the woman faced, was filled with compassion.

As the distraught woman came near to Jesus, He called out, "Do not weep." Then He took a step forward and touched the burial case of the young man. When He did this, the pallbearers stopped. Then Jesus said, "Young man, I say to you, arise!" At that, the deceased sat up and began to speak. Then Jesus motioned to the young man's mother to come over, and He gave her living son back to her. She was overwhelmed with joy.

The great joy of the mother was somewhat balanced with the fear that seized the crowd that witnessed all this. Many inwardly determined then and there to turn back to the Lord and live lives of love and compassion for others. Those who had remained faithful to the Lord, although shocked at the opportunity to see Jesus perform a miracle, were confirmed in their faith.

A great chorus of voices arose from the midst of the people proclaiming, "A great Prophet has risen among us." Some shouted, "God has visited His people." The news of this miracle spread throughout all of Judea and its surrounding region. In a sense, Jesus had matched all the prophets who had gone before. Also, Jesus exercised his power over death.

# JESUS CALMS THE STORM

*Luke 8:22-25*

AS Jesus' journeys took Him further and further from Capernaum, He and His followers were not always safe from His enemies and the sometimes natural consequences of travel in His time.

One time Jesus and His disciples arranged for a boat to take them across the Sea of Galilee. He had among His party a number of experienced fishermen and boat handlers. They knew the Sea of Galilee well and were quite adept at handling boats. Jesus therefore felt quite comfortable with His knowledgeable companions and had no trouble falling asleep while most of His friends tended sails as needed.

Like most inland seas, the Sea of Galilee was subject to sudden storms and squalls. Once the winds rose during a storm, the landbound water had no place toward which to flatten out. Thus, the once calm water could very rapidly grow into wildly dangerous seas. The boats in Jesus' day were not large and could, in a short time, become easy prey of the sea. The sailors on board with Jesus were all too familiar with the history of lost vessels on the Sea of Galilee.

With Jesus fast asleep, one of those sudden storms swept up into full fury in a short time. Despite the skills of the fishermen and sailors on board, the entire party became paralyzed with fear, thinking the boat was about to sink. They were rapidly taking on water and their bailing efforts seemed useless. They went to Jesus and woke Him up, shouting, "Master! Master! We are perishing!" As Jesus stumbled awake, finding it difficult to stand firm in the heavily pitching vessel, He spoke in a loud voice, commanding the wind and waves to recede. Immediately, Jesus was obeyed and a vast calm reappeared over the sea.

Jesus then spoke to His disciples with obvious disappointment and a slight hue of anger, saying, "Where is your faith?" A lack of faith on the part of His closest disciples was a trying experience for Jesus. The disciples did not answer Him. Still struggling with their fear, and, at the same time, a great sense of awe at Jesus' power, they continued to wonder as to the identity of the Master. With Jesus again resting in the bow of the boat, they said to one another in hushed voices, "Who can this be? He gives orders to the winds and the water, and they obey Him."

# JESUS CURES THE DEAF MAN

*Mark 7:31-37*

AFTER curing the possessed daughter of the Syrophoenician woman, when Jesus suggested His first concern was for Israelite peoples, and Gentiles second, He left the district of Tyre. Going through Sidon and over the Sea of Galilee, Jesus arrived in the District of Decapolis. Jesus, although somewhat exhausted from His journeys and preaching, gained some respite on the sea, but He found challenges and demands on His time due to His growing reputation as a healer and miracle worker.

Even though Decapolis and its surrounding area were inhabited mostly by Gentiles, the people there admittedly believed in Jesus' healing powers. There were times that seven others who claimed to be healers in the area took credit for Jesus' good works and deeds.

A group of people in Decapolis brought a deaf man to Jesus. The man also had a speech impediment. So the people begged Jesus to lay His hands on the deaf man. Perhaps they were sincere in their concern, or maybe they wanted to see a miracle. But Jesus "took him aside, away from the crowd." For a time before this moment, Jesus seems to have begun to practice performing miracles or healings in private. Jesus did not want people to recognize Him. He wanted the crowds to concentrate on His message rather than look for a spectacular event.

Alone with the deaf mute, He put his fingers into the man's ears and, spitting, touched his tongue; then He looked up to heaven and groaned, and said to him, *"Ephphatha!"* which means, "Be opened!" Right away the man could hear. His speech impediment was gone and he spoke so well that all could understand him. At the same time, Jesus ordered the people not to tell anyone. But the more He did so, the more they shouted the news. Despite Jesus' request and hope for secrecy, the people still recognized Him. News of Jesus continued to spread, especially about His healing power and miracles.

# JESUS HEALS THE MAN WITH THE WITHERED HAND

*Matthew 12:9-14*

AS Jesus moved further into His public life, He maintained a strict policy of adhering to Sabbath laws, especially worship in local community synagogues. On one Sabbath, as He and His disciples were going through a wheat field, some of the men were hungry and picked heads of grain and ate them. The Pharisees, who kept a tight watch on Jesus and His disciples, told Jesus that what He and His friends were doing was unlawful on the Sabbath. In reply, Jesus denied Sabbath laws were broken, proclaiming "For the Son of Man is Lord of the Sabbath."

From the field, Jesus and His friends went into the local synagogue as was their custom on the Sabbath. Inside the synagogue, there was a man with a withered hand. The Pharisees questioned Jesus saying, "Is it lawful to cure on the Sabbath?" They asked this of Jesus to trap Him. But Jesus, speaking to all assembled there, asked who there would not rescue one of his sheep if it fell into a ravine on the Sabbath. His question was greeted with silence. So, Jesus reminded the group how much more valuable a person is compared to a sheep.

Then Jesus told the man, "Stretch out your hand." He did so, and it was completely restored. The cure brought an end to the debate over Sabbath rules and observance. And the discussion had taken place in the Pharisees' own synagogue. This was a stinging rebuke for the Pharisees in the eyes of the people gathered there.

Jesus was actually teaching that if it is correct to save an animal on the Sabbath, how much more common sense does it make to cure or save a human being. The clear sincerity and love that came through in Jesus' words merely angered the Pharisees more. Almost immediately, they left the synagogue and spoke together against Jesus and about putting Him to death. In their minds, Jesus was assuming supreme authority over the law, and they would not tolerate this great disruption of their laws and traditions. Jesus heard of their plans to kill Him, and He and the disciples moved on to a different place.

# THE BEHEADING OF JOHN THE BAPTIST

*Mark 6:17-29*

NEWS of the many miracles and cures worked by Jesus reached Galilee and surrounding areas. It became the talk of the cities and villages, as well as travelers. Flatterers and informers informed King Herod of these stories. Still, for him, it all seemed to be remote in the security of his palace. However, when John the Baptist's words struck home, Herod became upset with both John and Jesus.

At one time, Herod had John the Baptist arrested and put in prison. Herod was married to Herodias, the wife of his brother Philip, who was still living when Herod married Herodias. John told Herod, "It is unlawful for you to have your brother's wife." John's words angered Herodias, who wanted to kill John, but could not do so. Herod realized John was a good and holy man, and, therefore, was fearful to give in to Herodias's death wish for John. Jail was about as far as Herod dared go. Surprisingly, Herod liked to listen to John, even though he was confused by what he said.

On Herod's birthday, he gave a banquet for his court attendants, military officers and some leading men of Galilee. Among the entertainers that evening was Herodias's daughter. She delighted Herod and his guests. He told the girl, "Ask me for whatever you wish, and I will give it to you." Some of the guests overheard the solemn promise of Herod, in which he said even if she asked for half of his kingdom, she would have it.

The girl went to her mother and wondered what she should ask for. Herodias told her to ask for the head of John the Baptist. She returned to the banquet room and told Herod, "I want you to give me at once the head of John the Baptist on a platter." Though the request upset Herod, he had taken an oath and he was afraid to break his word.

Immediately, Herod sent an executioner to bring back John's head. After executing John, he put the head on a platter. He returned to the banquet hall and gave everything to the girl, who handed it to Herodias. Herodias had her revenge in hand. When Jesus' disciples heard of John's death, they took his body and laid it in a tomb.

# THE MULTIPLICATION OF THE LOAVES AND FISH

*Mark 6:34-44*

JESUS wanted to take some time with His Apostles for prayer, rest and mutual support over concerns with their work. No matter what remote place they chose to meet in, the people followed.

When the Apostles and Jesus were finally all together, they were still in the presence of a large crowd. It reminded Jesus of a flock of sheep without a shepherd. So, with great patience, pity and compassion for the multitude, He taught them about God and the good news of the kingdom.

Eventually, the Apostles suggested to Jesus that the crowd should be dismissed. The sun was beginning to set, and there was little food available in the remote spot where they were. When the Apostles spoke to Jesus about the need for food, He said, "Give them something to eat yourselves." They answered in a frustrated tone, "Are we to buy two hundred days' wages worth of food and give it to them to eat?" He asked the Apostles to check around and see how much food was available. After combing the crowd, they reported there were five loaves and two fish on hand.

Jesus then ordered them to have the people sit in groups on the grass. They took their places in rows of fifties and hundreds. This arrangement recalled the groupings of their Israelite ancestors when they encamped in the desert.

Jesus took the five loaves and two fish, and raising His eyes and extending His arms to heaven, He prayed a blessing over the food. He began to break the bread and separated the two fish in readiness for distribution to the entire crowd. As the Apostles moved among the five thousand men, a multitude of women, and with some children present, the bread and fish did not run out. All ate and were satisfied. Then the Apostles went through the crowd, picking up the unwanted bread and fish. In all, they found twelve wicker baskets of uneaten food remaining.

All consumed food over which Jesus had said the traditional Jewish table ritual of blessing God before eating food. Many people near Jesus and the Apostles observed the amazing distribution of life-sustaining food that came from hardly enough to feed only the twelve Apostles.

# JESUS WALKS ON WATER

*Matthew 14:22-33*

AFTER the miracle of the loaves and fish, Jesus wanted His disciples to get into a boat and sail across the water to Bethsaida, a village at the northwestern shore of the Sea of Galilee. At the same time, Jesus made His way up the mountain. He wanted to spend some time in prayer alone.

The disciples were on their own as they crossed the Sea of Galilee. By nightfall, the boat was some distance out to sea. A sudden wind came up, which was no surprise to the experienced disciples. As time passed, the water became rougher and, given the strong headwinds, the disciples were having a difficult time controlling the boat. Still, they could row but were tiring quickly.

Jesus came down from the mountain. Standing on the shore, He could see the disciples' boat being tossed about. Battered by wind and wave, the disciples struggling at the oars at first could not believe their eyes. Jesus came walking across the sea in their direction. It seemed to them that His intention was to walk right past them. But when the disciples saw Him walking on water, they thought it was a ghost and cried out in fear.

Jesus stopped on the water, and shouted over the wind, "Have courage! It is I. Do not be afraid." Peter shouted back, "Lord, if it is You, command me to come to You across the water." "Come!" Jesus said. Peter got out of the boat and began to walk on the water toward Jesus. But, in a short time, he became frightened and began to sink. He yelled to Jesus, "Lord, save me!" Immediately, Jesus stretched out His arm and grabbed Peter. Then, in an almost angry tone, Jesus said to Peter, "How little faith you have. Why did you falter?"

Jesus and Peter got into the boat and the wind and sea calmed down. The others in the boat, who had been watching all this with astonishment, gave Jesus signs of reverence and awe, declaring, "Beyond doubt, You are the Son of God."

The disciples who had lived the multiplication of the loaves and fish still had a long way to grow in their faith. Likewise, in time of challenge, we can sometimes be lacking in faith. We want to walk across the waters of darkness and evil to the Lord, but the winds of temptation can easily frighten us.

# THE TRANSFIGURATION

*Mark 9:2-8*

AS Jesus hoped to lead His disciples to a fuller understanding of the role they would play in God's plan for the Messiah, He wanted to share at least some idea of the necessity of His passion so that all might be accomplished. After Jesus asked the question, "Who do people say I am?" He revealed the necessity of His death and Resurrection. If His chosen leaders understood this, Jesus wanted them to accept His invitation to walk with Him.

Almost as if to provide a balance for the disturbing news of Jesus' coming death and Resurrection, He took Peter, James and John and led them up onto a high mountain. When they reached a selected place, Jesus stopped, turned to the disciples and was transfigured in front of them. His clothes turned into a shade of white, "whiter than anyone on earth could bleach them." This was followed by absolute silence, so astonished were the disciples.

Suddenly, Elijah appeared with Moses, and they were speaking with Jesus. Then the disciples were struck with the awesome realization that the prophecy of Elijah and the law of Moses were accomplished as one in the person of Jesus. In his excitement and great enthusiasm. Peter said, "Rabbi, it is good for us to be here. Let us make three tents—one for You, one for Moses, and one for Elijah." There would be no tents. Still, Jesus' transfiguration made a deep impression on the disciples.

All of a sudden, "a cloud cast a shadow over them." At that moment, even the disciples entered into the mystery of Jesus' glorification. From the cloud came a loud voice saying, "This is My beloved Son. Listen to Him." And suddenly the disciples looked around and saw only Jesus standing there with them.

Then they started down the mountain. The disciples' minds were filled with wonder, and they were walking as if on air after their glimpse of glory. Without consulting one another, they seemed more determined than ever to follow Jesus wherever He would go, and do anything He asked. However, Jesus broke into their thoughts and urged them not to tell anyone what they had seen, "until the Son of Man had risen from the dead." They still were not sure what rising from the dead meant.

# JESUS AND THE CHILDREN

*Mark 9:33-37*

AS time passed and Jesus continued His public ministry, He faced the ongoing challenge of helping His disciples understand their need to grow according to God's word. They were called to be leaders. Therefore, they had to try to move away from personal interests to a more universal approach to life and spiritual growth.

Sometimes Jesus' disciples exhibited degrees of ambition that could hinder their pastoral cause. They would argue over who among them was most important. Jesus addressed this issue in a very clear and firm manner. Once, when Jesus and all the disciples were gathered in the house at Capernaum, He asked them, "What were you arguing about during the journey?" No one answered. They were too ashamed to speak because they were discussing who was most qualified in the group. Jesus was upset with them, so He sat them down and spoke to them like a father. "If anyone wishes to be first, he must become the last of all and the servant of all."

He then invited a child in who had been playing nearby. He asked the lad to stand in the middle of the seated disciples. Then He put His arms around him and said, "Whoever receives one such child in My name receives Me; and whoever receives Me receives not Me but the One Who sent Me."

Jesus was clearly telling the disciples that their role in His work was to be one of service, especially to the poor and rejected. Given the social customs of his day, Jesus used children as a symbol of the poor in spirit, the lowly in the community. Unfortunately, children were considered to be of no significance at that time, and since in law they had no rights, many adults had little respect for them.

As Jesus traveled about during His public life, He always took an interest in the children who were present. And He would make sure to take time to be with them and listen to their hopes, fears and joys. So, wherever He went, people would bring their children to Him. Once when Jesus was tired, the disciples tried to keep the children from Him. Jesus saw this, and scolded His disciples, saying, "Let the little children come to Me, and do not hinder them. For it is to such as these that the kingdom of heaven belongs."

# THE GOOD SAMARITAN

*Luke 10:29-37*

ONCE when Jesus was out preaching, an expert in Mosaic law asked him, "Teacher, what must I do to gain eternal life?" Jesus asked him what the law stated and how he understood it. So the young man answered, "You shall love the Lord your God with all your heart, and with all your soul, and with all your strength, and with all your mind, and your neighbor as yourself." Jesus congratulated him for his fine answer, and told him if he followed the law he would live forever.

But he asked Jesus, "And who is my neighbor?" Jesus then told the young man and the crowd gathered there about a man who was traveling from Jerusalem to Jericho. He was attacked by a gang of thieves who stripped him of his clothing and anything else of value he had on his person. In the process, he was physically beaten almost to death. Then the robbers hurried away, leaving the man lying along the roadside.

A priest, who would have been expected to be a model of neighborliness, came along. He saw the beaten man but continued along on the other side of the road. The same neighborly concern would have been expected of a Levite who came along and saw the victim but passed by.

Eventually, a Samaritan traveler came down the road and saw the crumpled body. He was filled with compassion for the stripped, injured man. He knelt by the victim and determined he was still alive. The Samaritan cleansed and bandaged the open wounds. After resting a moment, the Samaritan was able to lift the victim onto his animal and took him to a nearby inn where he cared for him. Following a restful night, the Samaritan gave the innkeeper silver coins and said, "Look after him, and when I return I will repay you for anything more you might spend." Then Jesus addressed the young scholar and the crowd, asking, "Which of those three, do you think, was a neighbor to him who fell among thieves?" Almost shamefaced, the lawyer said, "The one who showed him mercy." Jesus replied, "Go and do likewise."

Some of the Jewish people there were shocked at Jesus' words. They always considered the Samaritans to be enemies, not neighbors. The lesson was simple: We are to have compassion for all people.

# THE PRODIGAL SON

*Luke 15:11-32*

AS Jesus moved further along in His public ministry, He was trying to accomplish specific goals. He wanted His followers to realize how concerned He and the Father were over those who lost their way to the kingdom, and, at the same time, how great was the Father's love for repentant sinners.

Jesus wanted the scribes, Pharisees, and all to come to an understanding of the mercy of God. So He taught the parable of the prodigal son. A young man and his brother worked with their father on a large family farm. However, the young son had a great desire to leave the farm and go out on his own. Therefore, he asked his father for his portion of the family wealth, which he was due to inherit. Reluctantly, the father agreed to this and figured what his son's share of the estate would be.

Once he received his money, the young son packed his belongings and left the homestead. He settled in a "distant country." It did not take him long to acquire many friends since people realized he had money. He spent freely and recklessly, living a wild lifestyle. Never thinking he would run out of money, he soon was destitute and without friends. Then a famine struck the land, and he was able only to hire out to one of the local people to tend his swine, which ate better than he.

In great distress, he realized the servants on his father's farm were better off. So he decided to go home and ask to stay there as a servant. His father saw him coming and ran to embrace him. He said, "Father, I have sinned against heaven and against you. I am no longer worthy to be called your son." In response his father ordered new clothes, sandals and a ring for him. A fatted calf was prepared. Why did the father do this? "For this son of mine was dead and has come back to life." Then the feast began.

At nightfall, the older son returning from the fields, heard the party and was told his brother had returned. Angered, he would not go in. His father pleaded with him. But he complained he had remained faithful yet was never allowed to celebrate with his friends. The father replied, "Son, you are with me always, and everything I have is yours. But we should celebrate . . . because this brother of yours was dead and has come to life; he was lost and now he has been found."

# JESUS RAISES LAZARUS

*John 11:1-44*

WHEN Jesus was preaching in the area of the Jordan River, a messenger interrupted Him with the news that a good friend of His was ill. It was Lazarus, the brother of Martha and Mary. Jesus waited another two days before He started out to visit Lazarus and his sisters.

He shared His plans to go to Bethany with the disciples. But they were apprehensive because some Jewish people in the area were upset with Jesus and had tried to stone Him to death. So, they took the precaution of traveling at night. Then He told His disciples that Lazarus was asleep, but He meant Lazarus was dead. He then explained, "I am glad for your sake that I was not there, so that you may believe. Let us go to him." Jesus implied He would raise Lazarus from the dead.

When Jesus arrived in Bethany, He found Lazarus had been dead for four days. Many Jewish people had come to Martha and Mary's home to comfort them. When Martha heard Jesus was coming she ran out to meet Him, saying, "Lord, if You had been here, my brother would not have died." Jesus told her, "Your brother will rise again." Martha agreed he would rise on the last day. However, Jesus replied, "I am the resurrection and the life. Whoever believes in Me, even though he dies, will live, and everyone who lives and believes in Me will never die." Jesus asked Martha if she believed this and she said, "Yes, Lord. I believe that You are the Christ, the Son of God."

Martha ran back home to get Mary. The Jewish people sitting there got up and followed them, thinking they were going to Lazarus's tomb. But they returned to Jesus, and Mary fell at Jesus' feet, saying her brother would have lived had He been there. Her tears upset Jesus, and He asked where they put Lazarus. At the sight of Lazarus's tomb, Jesus wept. The Jewish people said, "See how greatly He loved him!" Others wondered if Jesus could cure the blind, why He couldn't do something here.

Then Jesus ordered the stone to the tomb removed. Jesus raised His eyes and said, "Father, I thank You for hearing Me." Then He cried out, "Lazarus, come out!" And Lazarus obeyed. He was covered in burial bands, and his face was wrapped in a cloth. Jesus said, "Untie him and let him go free."

# JESUS ENTERS JERUSALEM

*Luke 19:28-40*

AS Jesus' public ministry was coming to an end, He and His disciples started toward Jerusalem. At the Mount of Olives, Jesus sent two of His disciples on ahead into a nearby village. He told them they would find a colt there that had never been ridden. They were to untie the colt and bring it to Jesus.

They did as Jesus told them. Everything was just as He had explained. The owner of the colt caught the disciples and asked, "Why are you untying it?" And they answered just as Jesus had told them, saying, "The Lord needs it."

Then the disciples threw their cloaks over the colt and helped Jesus to sit astride the animal. As Jesus rode along, the people were surprised to see Him riding rather than walking as usual. In light of Jesus' popularity, the people began to lay their cloaks over the road on which He rode. This was a sign of great respect. Other people cut branches from palm trees and spread them on the road, waving them in honor of Jesus and His party as if He were a king.

Recalling all the wonders Jesus had worked, along with His compassion and understanding, the crowds seemed swept up in the emotion of the moment shouting, "Blessed is the King Who comes in the name of the Lord. Peace in heaven and glory in the highest heavens." Their shouted praise was really an expression of hope that salvation would be achieved in a short time in the city of Jerusalem. At the same time, others in the city were startled, for they heard the noise of the crowd following and welcoming Jesus. The newness of the situation left both the religious and the political leaders confused and uncertain.

The Pharisees said to Jesus, "Teacher, rebuke Your disciples." Jesus replied, "I tell you, if they keep silent, the stones would cry out." Even the Pharisees felt the public display of praise and rejoicing was not typical of Jesus. So when they asked Jesus to settle the people down over this, His short reply was full of meaning.

Jesus, Who formerly challenged His disciples not to speak or allow any activity that would hint at His role as Messiah, is now refusing to dampen their enthusiasm. For Jesus, it was now time for all to realize and acknowledge His role as Messiah.

# THE LAST SUPPER

*Luke 22:1-20; John 13:1-30*

THE Thursday after Jesus' arrival in Jerusalem, it was time to celebrate the great Passover meal. Jesus sent two disciples into the city, telling them they would see a man carrying a water jar, and they were to follow him. No matter which house he entered, they were to go in there and ask the owner where the Teacher's guest room was so He could eat the Passover meal there. The owner showed the disciples a large, furnished room on the second floor.

They returned to Jesus and reported all was in readiness as He said it would be. Once Jesus and the Apostles arrived, everything would be prepared according to custom. The thirteen assembled in the designated room. Jesus got up from the table, took off His cloak and wrapped a towel around His waist. He took a water jar and began washing the Apostles' feet.

Peter was upset at this, and when Jesus came to him, he strongly objected. Jesus calmly told Peter, "Unless I wash you, you will have no share with Me." The remorseful Peter asked to have his head and hands washed also, but Jesus said it was not nec-essary. Then Jesus announced to the disciples, "If I, your Lord and Teacher, have washed your feet, you also should wash one anoth-er's feet."

Jesus then returned to the table and said, "I have eagerly desired to eat this Passover with you before I suffer. For I tell you I shall never eat again until it is fulfilled in the kingdom of God." He took a cup, gave thanks to the Father and said, "Take this and share it among yourselves. For I tell you that from this moment I shall not drink of the fruit of the vine until the kingdom of God comes." He also took bread, prayed a blessing, broke the bread and gave it to the disciples, saying, "This is My body, which will be given for you. Do this in memory of Me." After they ate the bread He gave them the cup, saying, "This cup is the new covenant in My blood, which will be poured out for you." This was the first Eucharist.

Jesus then told the disciples one of their number would betray Him. Peter signaled John to find out who it was. Jesus dipped a morsel in wine and gave it to Judas Iscariot, and said to him, "Do quickly what you are going to do." Judas left at once.

# THE AGONY IN THE GARDEN

*Matthew 26:31-46; Luke 22:31-34, 39-46*

AT the end of the Passover meal, Jesus told His disciples, "All of you will have your faith tested." Peter replied that even if the others were shaken in their faith, he would not break down. Then Jesus predicted Peter would shortly deny he knew Him.

Leaving the Upper Room with Jesus, they went to a garden nearby called Gethsemane. He said to the disciples, "Sit here while I go and pray." Then He took Peter, James and John a little further. He seemed to be in great distress and told the three, "My soul is sorrowful even to the point of death. Remain here and keep watch." Jesus went a few steps further and then fell to the ground in prayer. He asked His Father if the hour of His death could pass Him by. He said, "My Father, if it is possible, allow this cup to be taken from Me. Yet let Your will, not Mine, be done."

When He returned to the disciples, He found them asleep. He said to Peter, "Could you not keep watch with Me for just one hour? Stay awake and pray that you may not enter into temptation. The spirit is indeed willing, but the flesh is weak." Then Jesus left again and prayed as He had before. When He went back to the three a second time, they were sleeping. The same thing happened a third time and Jesus said, "Are you still sleeping and taking your rest? Behold, the hour has come for the Son of Man to be betrayed into the hands of sinners. Get up! Let us be going. Look, My betrayer is approaching."

When Jesus first began to pray in the garden, His humanity surfaced in His fear of death. Yet, He was able to accept the Father's will for the good of all peoples. He accepted all that would happen to Him so that everyone would have salvation available.

While Jesus was still speaking to the disciples in the garden, Judas Iscariot appeared with a hostile crowd carrying swords and clubs. Sent by the chief priests, scribes and elders, they had been searching for Jesus. Judas had beforehand arranged a signal as to which of the thirteen was Jesus. "The one I shall kiss is the man. Arrest Him." So, Judas went right up to Jesus and addressed Him as "Rabbi" and kissed Him. Then Jesus was arrested right away, and He went peacefully.

# "BEHOLD THE MAN"

*Matthew 27:1-31; John 18:1—19:16*

AS Jesus was being led out of the Garden of Gethsemane, the disciples fled. Jesus' captors took Him before the Sanhedrin, where the chief priests, elders and the entire Sanhedrin looked for false testimony against Him. Finally, two men said they heard Jesus say He could destroy God's temple and build it again in three days. The leaders asked Jesus to reply to this, but He would not. So the high priest ordered Jesus to take an oath as to whether He was the Son of God. Jesus replied, "You have said it."

The high priest tore his garment, asserting Jesus had blasphemed. Others said He deserved to die. Then they spit on His face and slapped Him. The following morning, Jesus was bound and taken to Pilate, the governor. Standing before Pilate, Jesus was questioned, "Are You the King of the Jews?" Jesus said, "You have said so." When the chief priests and elders brought accusations against Him, He kept silent. When Pilate asked Him if He had anything to say of the testimony against Him, He remained silent.

It was the custom of the governor to release a prisoner on Passover. He took Jesus out on the balcony and proclaimed, "Behold the Man." Then he asked if he should free Jesus or Barabbas, a notorious criminal. The chief priests and elders urged the people to ask for Barabbas. And Pilate asked the crowd, "What shall I do with the Messiah, called Jesus?" The people shouted, "Let Him be crucified." Pilate answered, "Why? What evil has He done?" The people shouted louder, "Let Him be crucified." Pilate told them he was innocent of Jesus' blood. Their reply was, "Let His blood be on us and on our children."

Pilate came back out to the governor's chair and washed his hands, removing, in his mind, any responsibility for shedding Jesus' blood. After he had Jesus scourged, his soldiers took Him to the praetorium, where they stripped off His clothes and placed a purple military cloak on Him. Then they made a crown of large thorns for His head, pushing it down into His flesh. A reed was placed in His right hand, mocking His kingly power. They genuflected before Jesus, mockingly calling Him "King of the Jews." Then they led out Jesus to be crucified.

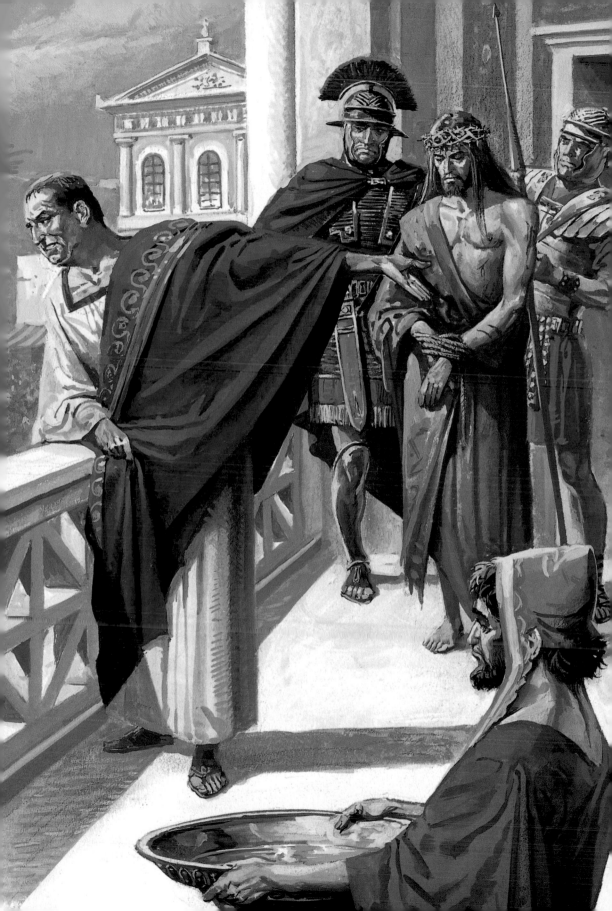

# JESUS CARRIES HIS CROSS

*Luke 23:26-32*

WHEN Jesus started His walk toward Calvary, where He would be put to death, there was an unusual development. It was decided that Jesus would be required to carry part of His Cross. It was customary for others condemned to die by crucifixion, both a horror and a death of public disgrace, to be walked to the spot of crucifixion and then placed on the cross.

So, when Jesus had the crosspiece of His Cross placed on His shoulder outside the praetorium, it was an additional mark of humiliation and mockery for Him. He was to be treated as the lowest of the low by making Him struggle with the heavy wood on the way to His horrific death.

Those in charge of the procession to the place of crucifixion also carried a sign ordered by Pilate to be attached to Jesus' Cross when He was lifted up. It read, "Jesus the Nazorean, King of the Jews." This was, on Pilate's part, an ironic title of accusation against Jesus. Even though he used the term, he was totally aware of the evil motives of the chief priests who handed over Jesus for trial and condemnation. When the chief priests and elders protested how the sign read, Pilate replied, "What I have written, I have written."

As Jesus carried His Cross, He met His distraught Mother, who was all too aware of the pain, suffering and humiliation her only Son was enduring. At the same time, other women and children who were there wept at the sight of Jesus. Ever compassionate, Jesus told them not to weep for Him but for themselves and for their children.

As Jesus moved along slowly, He weakened under the burden of the heavy wood, and His lack of food, water and loss of blood. As a result, He would fall. The soldiers would curse and beat Him until He got up. Yet, the soldiers worried they would be in trouble if Jesus died before reaching Calvary. They saw a man coming in from the fields and forced him to help carry the Cross. He was Simon of Cyrene.

At the top of a hill called Golgotha, the soldiers stripped Jesus, tearing open His wounds. He was nailed on the Cross that had been put together. The Cross was raised and dropped into a hole, causing terrible pain for Jesus.

# JESUS DIES ON THE CROSS

*Luke 23:33-49*

WHEN the procession following Jesus to Calvary reached its destination, Jesus was nailed to the Cross. Jesus would hang on the Cross, between two thieves being crucified at the same time, for a number of hours.

Jesus said, "Father, forgive them, for they do not know what they do." Ordinary foot soldiers and unbelievers in the crowd had little understanding or realization of the divinity of Jesus and the blasphemy of His being put to death.

When the soldiers realized Jesus had been wearing a seamless garment, instead of dividing it, they drew straws for it. Some local leaders sneered at Jesus saying, "He saved others. Let Him save Himself if He is the Christ of God, the Chosen One." But how could they have known Jesus already accepted the Father's will and would not save Himself and lose salvation for all? The soldiers, imitating their leaders, jeered Jesus and mockingly offered Him bitter wine to quench His thirst.

One of the robbers hanging with Jesus snarled at Him that if He was the Messiah He should save all three men on their crosses. The second thief scolded the first for having no fear of God, saying Jesus was innocent but they were guilty. Then he asked Jesus to remember him when He came into His kingdom. Jesus replied, "Amen, I say to you, this day you will be with Me in Paradise." Standing at the foot of His Cross, although closely guarded by a soldier, was Mary, Jesus' Mother, and John, His close friend and disciple. Jesus knew His Mother's heart was breaking seeing Him suffer so. He said to her, "Woman, behold your son," meaning John, and to His friend, "Behold your Mother." From then on, John cared for her in a special way.

Around noon the world darkened due to an eclipse of the sun until three in the afternoon. Then the veil of the temple was torn down the middle. Jesus cried out in a loud voice, "Father, into Your hands I commend My spirit." And He drew His final breath.

People gathered at the foot of the Cross stood transfixed in horrified silence. A centurion who saw what happened broke the silence, proclaiming in a loud voice Jesus' innocence. It was a great leap of faith that could have cost him his life. Peace prevailed.

# JESUS IS CARRIED TO HIS TOMB

*Matthew 27:57-61; Mark 15:42-47; Luke 23:50-56; John 19:31-42*

WHEN Jesus died, there was much confusion on Calvary and in the praetorium. In both places, religious and political leaders were making sure their plans concerning Jesus were carried out to the fullest extent of the law. Since it was nearly sundown, the official beginning of the Sabbath, a holyday for the Jewish people, major issues had to be settled.

There was concern the bodies might remain on the crosses. Jesus died before the two thieves and, to hasten their deaths, the soldiers broke their legs. When they saw Jesus was already dead, one soldier pierced His side with a spear. Blood and water flowed out. All this happened as it had been written in Scripture: "A bone of His shall not be broken." And, "They shall look on Him Whom they have pierced."

There was a virtuous and righteous man, Joseph of Arimathea, who was a council member who did not consent to the plan against Jesus. Putting himself in possible danger, Joseph went to Pilate and begged to let him have the body of Jesus. Pilate, although not Jewish, likewise wanted the bodies down and readily agreed to allow Joseph to take possession of Jesus' body.

With the help of Nicodemus, a Pharisee and member of the Sanhedrin, he removed Jesus' body from the Cross. Then they wrapped it in linen cloth and carried it to a nearby garden. The garden had not yet been used as a cemetery. However, Joseph had made a tomb there for himself. It was carved out of rock.

As was the Jewish custom, spices were added to the linen before the body was wrapped up. The banded body was then placed on a slab in the tomb, and a large rock was placed in front of the vault. The women from Galilee who had followed Jesus to Calvary watched the burial. When they saw where Jesus was placed, they went home and prepared more spices and perfumed oils, planning to return after the Sabbath.

In the meantime, the chief priests and Pharisees hurried to see Pilate. They reminded him Jesus had said while He was alive that He would come back to life in three days. They asked Pilate to guard the tomb so Jesus' disciples could not steal the body and claim Jesus was risen. Pilate, somewhat annoyed, told them to guard the tomb themselves, and so they did.

# THE RESURRECTION

*Matthew 28:1-10; Mark 16:1-11; Luke 24:1-12; John 20:1-18*

EARLY the day following the Sabbath, the soldiers whom the chief priests and elders had sent to guard the tomb were thrown into confusion and fear as a tremendous flash of blinding light came from inside the tomb. Amid a great rumbling sound, the stone in front of the tomb rolled back. Jesus came out, clothed in white.

In the meantime, at the first sign of dawn, some women gathered spices, intending to go to the tomb and anoint Jesus' body. As they approached the tomb, they were saying to one another, "Who will roll back the stone for us from the entrance to the tomb?" When they were very close to the place, they noticed the large stone had already been moved. They entered the tomb and saw a young man sitting on the right side, dressed all in white. This upset them. He tried to calm them, saying, "Do not be afraid! You are looking for Jesus of Nazareth, Who was crucified. He has been raised. See the place where they laid Him. Go tell His disciples and Peter, 'He is going ahead of you to Galilee. There you will see Him just as He told you.' "

All this was too much for the women. They backed out bewildered and fled the cemetery. Still, Mary of Magdala who had seen the empty tomb hastened to tell Peter and the disciples. So, Peter and the younger disciple ran to the tomb to see what, if anything, had happened. The young disciple arrived first. He looked in and saw the burial wrappings and the piece of linen that covered Jesus' face. But they were separated. When Peter arrived, he went in followed by the other disciple. He saw and believed. There was no sign of the body, so they returned home.

Mary Magdalene stood weeping outside the tomb since she thought someone had stolen the body of Jesus. She decided to enter the tomb and saw two Angels sitting there. They asked why she was weeping. She explained that the body of Jesus had been taken and she had no idea where it was.

After leaving the tomb, she saw a man walking in the garden. He asked why she was crying and whom she was looking for. She asked if he had taken the body. He said, "Mary." She recognized Him and cried, "Rabboni," meaning teacher.

# DOUBTING THOMAS

*John 20:19-29*

AS different rumors of Jesus' Resurrection began to move among the people like lightning, the Apostles, wanting to know the complete story, made their individual ways to the Upper Room where they had celebrated Passover with Jesus. It was at first a secret affair, with the Apostles gathering one by one, and as each entered, the door was securely barricaded behind him. They were really in hiding for fear of some Jewish people who were angry with them, thinking they and their followers had stolen Jesus' body and hid it somewhere so they could spread the news that Jesus had risen from the dead.

As the sun began to set that Sunday, Jesus came through the locked door and said to the Apostles, "Peace be with you." Then He showed them where His hands, feet and side had been wounded. The Apostles were ecstatic with joy, praising the Lord in the confirmed knowledge that He had risen from the dead. Again the Lord said, "Peace be with you."

Then Jesus came very close to the disciples and breathed on them and said, "Receive the Holy Spirit. If you forgive sins, they are forgiven. If you retain sins, they are retained."

One of the eleven, Thomas, also called Didymus, was not there when Jesus appeared that Easter evening. When Thomas did join them, the disciples told him they had seen the Lord. But he said, "Unless I see the mark of the nails on His hands and put my finger into the place where the nails pierced and insert my hand into His side, I will not believe."

The following Sunday, when all the Apostles, including Thomas, were gathered in the Upper Room, Jesus again passed through the locked door and stood in the middle of the Apostles. Jesus said to them, "Peace be with you." Then He said to Thomas, "Put your finger here and see My hands. Reach out your hand and put it into My side. Do not doubt any longer, but believe." The other Apostles watched in awed silence to see what Thomas's response would be. Thomas said to Jesus, "My Lord and my God!" While Jesus could have humiliated Thomas in front of the others, or scolded him because of his unbelief, His response was gentle. "You have come to believe because you have seen Me. Blessed are those who have not seen and yet have come to believe." Jesus' words to Thomas are a central teaching for all the baptized. As the followers of Christ live their lives, walking with Him and the Father, they will endure challenges to their faith regarding the Resurrection of Jesus from the dead.

# THE ASCENSION

*Luke 24:50-53; Acts 1:1-12*

AS a part of our Church calendar, we recall that forty days following Jesus' Resurrection from the dead, He ascended into heaven. When Jesus returned to the Father, He was in effect teaching us that we too will go to the Father. But at first, we will be without our bodies, which will remain in the earth until the end of the world.

Between the time of His Resurrection and His return home to the Father, Jesus seemed to the Apostles to be rather elusive. However, in many ways, Jesus presented Himself alive to the Apostles. He met with Thomas and invited Thomas to touch His wounds; He ate baked fish with the disciples in the Upper Room; and He breathed on them when He first met them in the Upper Room. Over those forty days following His Resurrection, Jesus appeared to the Apostles speaking to them about the kingdom of God.

Near the end of forty days, Jesus told His disciples not to leave Jerusalem, but to "wait there for the promise of the Father about which you have heard Me speak. For John baptized with water, but within a few days you will be baptized with the Holy Spirit." The Apostles asked Jesus if He was going to restore the kingdom of Israel. This implied that while they believed Jesus was the Christ, they expected Him to be a political leader Who would restore self-rule to Israel. They were asking if it was to occur then. But Jesus wanted them to focus on the beginnings of the Church, since Jesus would ascend to the Father, and the Apostles would be in charge.

Jesus told the Apostles they would receive power when the "Holy Spirit comes upon you, and then you will be My witnesses not only in Jerusalem . . . and indeed to the farthest ends of the earth." Jesus assured the Apostles that as the foundation of His Church, the Holy Spirit would be the source of all the wisdom and power they would need to lead the Church.

Then Jesus lifted up His arms and, blessing the Apostles, He was lifted up, "and a cloud took Him from their sight." Suddenly, two men dressed in white were standing there. They said, "Men of Galilee, why are you standing there looking up into the sky? This Jesus Who has been taken up from you into heaven will come back in the same way as you have seen Him going into heaven."

# THE DESCENT OF
# THE HOLY SPIRIT

*Acts 1:13—2:13*

AFTER a day's journey from the Mount of Olives, the Apostles went to the Upper Room in Jerusalem. All eleven were there. They devoted themselves to prayer. During that time, Peter announced the death of Judas on some land he had purchased.

It was necessary for Judas's replacement to be elected. It had to be one who followed Jesus during His entire public ministry. Two were chosen: Joseph, called Barsabbas, and Matthias. Following a time of prayer the Apostles voted, and Matthias was chosen.

When the time arrived for Pentecost, all the Apostles were together. Suddenly, a loud noise startled them. It sounded like a strong-driven wind, a signal from God that He was about to interact with the Apostles in a special way. Tongues, which seemed to the Apostles to be fire, appeared and settled on each of them. While fire symbolized the presence of the Holy Spirit, here it was clear that God was acting upon the Apostles in such a way as to prepare them to preach the new covenant between God and His people.

The Apostles were filled with the Holy Spirit, and they began to speak in different languages. These languages indicated their call to bring the good news to peoples all over the world. It was a reaffirmation of Jesus' announcement that the Apostles would be challenged in their mission to go to all corners of the earth.

At Pentecost in Jerusalem, devout Jewish people came to celebrate. Due to the loud noise, they gathered outside the Apostles' house. The Apostles, now filled with the Holy Spirit, went out to them. The people became confused since they soon realized the Apostles were speaking in their language. They said to one another, "Are not all these men who are speaking Galileans?" They wondered among themselves what this meant.

Peter stood up with all the Apostles and said, "These men are not drunk, as you suppose." Then he reminded them of the prophet Joel who said God would send His Spirit on all peoples and work wonders on earth. He recalled for the Israelites how David spoke of the Resurrection of a Messiah. Afterward, three thousand repented and asked for baptism.

# PETER, THE FIRST POPE

*John 21:1-19; Acts 10:34*

SOME disciples, Peter, Thomas, Nathaniel, James, John and a few others were near the Sea of Tiberias. Peter said, "I am going out to fish." They all agreed to go. They fished most of the night but were unsuccessful. Around dawn, standing on the shore, Jesus appeared. At first, they did not realize it was Jesus. He asked if they had caught anything. When they answered no, Jesus suggested they fish off the right side of the boat.

They did so, and in a short time had a large catch. Then the disciples realized it was Jesus standing on the shore. John cried out, "It is the Lord." Peter waded ashore. The others followed.

Onshore, they saw Jesus had prepared breakfast for them. He told them to bring some of the fish they caught, and He would prepare the meal, along with the fish and bread that He already prepared.

During all this, although the disciples were somewhat sure, they did not dare ask, "Who are You?" What convinced them that it was Jesus was the manner in which He distributed the bread and fish. For them, it recalled the Passover meal. This was the third time Jesus had revealed Himself to the disciples since the Resurrection.

When the meal finished, Jesus said to Peter, "Do you love Me more than these?" Peter said, "Yes, Lord, You know that I love You." Jesus replied, "Feed My sheep." A second time Jesus said, "Simon, son of John, do you love Me?" Peter said, "Yes, Lord, You know that I love You." Jesus replied, "Tend My sheep." A third time Jesus said, "Simon, son of John, do you love Me?" This upset Peter since it was the third time. Peter replied, "You know everything. You know that I love You." Jesus said, "Feed My sheep." Then Jesus predicted the kind of death Peter would experience once he grew old.

According to the teaching of the First Vatican Council, the dialogue between Peter and Jesus made Peter leader as the supreme shepherd and ruler over Jesus' entire flock. In the Church today, we recognize the Pope as supreme ruler and direct descendant of St. Peter. Later, Peter declared, "I now understand how true it is that God has no favorites." The Church of Jesus is open to all without exception.

# BIBLE DICTIONARY

**Aaron.** Member of the tribe of Levi, brother of Moses and his spokesman before Pharaoh. He was chosen by God as the first high priest of the Old Law.

**Abel.** The religious and just son of Adam and Eve whose sacrifice pleased God yet aroused the murderous envy of his brother Cain. He was a shepherd and offered the firstlings of his flock to the Lord.

**Abraham.** "Father of believers." At God's command he left his home in Ur of the Chaldees about 2000 B.C. and settled in Palestine. God made a covenant with him and promised him a great posterity. In his old age his wife Sarah bore him a son (Isaac) in fulfillment of God's promise.

**Adam.** The first man created by God out of dust of the ground. In Hebrew "man" is *adam* and "the ground" is *adamah*.

**Altar.** A stone or pile of stones, or any structure or place on which sacrifices were burned or incense offered.

**Amen.** A Hebrew word meaning "firmly" or "surely," prefixed by Christ to statements of special solemnity.

**Angels of God.** Pure spirits created by God without bodies, completely independent of matter, who act as messengers or ambassadors of God.

**Annas.** Father-in-law of Caiaphas, the high priest at the time of Christ.

**Apostles.** Twelve men chosen by Christ to enjoy special jurisdiction and to teach. They are Peter, Andrew, James, John, Philip. Bartholomew, Thomas, Matthew, James the Less, Jude, Simon the Zealot, and Judas, who was replaced by Matthias.

**Ark of Noah.** A rectangular vessel built by Noah, in which he, his family, his possessions and some animals were preserved during the Flood.

**Ark of the Covenant.** The chest of wood covered with gold which contained the stone Tablets with the Ten Commandments written on them.

**Assyria.** A country occupying the northern and middle part of Mesopotamia, including Babylonia and Chaldea. The Assyrians were probably of Semitic origin, descendants of Asshur, one of the sons of Shem. An independent kingdom began about the seventeenth century B.C. In 606 B.C. Nineveh was destroyed by the Medes and Babylonians, and Assyria became a province of these countries.

**Baal.** The chief god of the Canaanites and the Phoenicians; the word meant "lord."

**Babylon.** Capital of Babylonia, to which many Jewish captives were deported after the fall of Jerusalem in 586 B.C.; this is known as the Babylonian Captivity.

**Banquet.** A feast at which abundant good food was served. Christ told the parable of a great Supper or Banquet.

**Beatitudes.** Eight blessings pronounced by our Lord at the beginning of the Sermon on the Mount.

**Bethlehem.** Place of Christ's birth, six miles south of Jerusalem.

**Blessing.** Used for: (1) bestowal of divine favor; (2) man's praise of and thanksgiving to God; (3) invocation of divine favor for man by man.

**Bronze Serpent.** A serpent of bronze made by Moses at God's command that saved all those who looked at it from the bites of poisonous snakes.

**Cain.** First son of Adam and Eve and murderer of his brother Abel.

**Caiaphas.** Jewish High Priest at the time of our Lord, who prophesied His death through the Holy Spirit.

**Captivity.** State of mankind after Adam's sin, symbolized by the captivity of the Jews in Egypt and Babylonia.

**Centurion.** Officer in charge of a **century** (originally 100 men), sixtieth part of the Roman legion. Legionnaires in Palestine were recruited locally, but officers were Roman.

**Cherubim.** Angels entrusted with important functions in the Bible: they were stationed as guardians at the gates of paradise after the expulsion of Adam and Eve (Genesis 3:24); Moses placed two cherubim on the cover of the Ark of the Covenant (Exodus 25:18).

**Chosen People.** Applies to Israelites (descendants of Abraham) who were chosen by God from many peoples by virtue of His promise to Abraham.

**Christ.** A name given to the Incarnate Word meaning "The Anointed One" or "The Messiah." This was His official title and revealed to the Jews that He was the King and Redeemer Whom they awaited. Jesus, which means 'the Lord is salvation" or "Savior," is His personal name and denotes His mission: to save human beings from death and sin; make them once more children of God and heirs of heaven.

**Circumcision.** A religious rite chosen by God to be the external sign of the Covenant God made with Abraham and all his descendants. In the New Covenant, it is replaced by baptism, which marks with a spiritual and indelible sign Christians who are spiritual descendants of Abraham.

**Commandments, The Ten.** Given by God to Moses on two stone Tablets. Christ gave us the two greatest Commandments of the Law.

**Covenant. Old:** Agreement between God and the Jewish people through the mediation of Moses. **New:** Agreement between God and all people through the Mediator, Jesus Christ.

**Cup.** Vessel used for drinking and for the thanksgiving offering of wine. At times it may refer to one's destiny.

**Cyrus.** King of Persia, who conquered Babylonia and freed the Jews from their Babylonian Captivity.

**Dagon.** Originally, a Mesopotamian deity whom the Philistines came to worship as their own god of grain.

**Damascus.** Capital of Syria, destroyed in 732 B.C., which had a large Jewish population.

**Daniel.** The hero of the Book of the Bible that bears his name and one of the four Major Prophets. He lived during the Babylonian Exile.

**Darkness.** Absence of light. In the Bible God, Who is eternal truth, is considered the true light and the source of all light; therefore darkness becomes a symbol of estrangement from God. Jesus said that those who followed Him would not walk in darkness (John 8:12), i.e., He would show them clearly the truth.

**David.** The youngest son of Jesse and second King of United Israel. The prophet Nathan foretold that the Messiah would be a descendant of David.

**Day of the Lord.** Described often in prophetical writings, it generally signified the Coming of the Lord in power and majesty to destroy His enemies and inaugurate His Kingdom. Sometimes called the **Last Day** or simply **that Day.**

**Devil(s).** The name given to angels who rebelled against God under the leadership of Satan.

**Dove.** A bird of the pigeon family, which has been chosen to be a symbol of the Holy Spirit, probably because of its gentleness and purity.

**Elijah.** The dramatic 9th century B.C. Hebrew prophet who fought against the idolatry in Israel during the reign of the wicked King Ahab. He worked many wonders and was taken to heaven in a fiery chariot. Jesus said that John the Baptist resembled Elijah in spirit and in power (Matthew 11:14).

**Elisha.** Friend and disciple of Elijah who took his place as prophet after Elijah's ascension.

**Epistle.** A letter.

**Esau.** Elder brother of Jacob who sold his heritage to the latter for a mess of pottage; ancestor of the Edomites.

**Evangelist.** Name given to the writers of the inspired Message brought by Jesus. They are sometimes depicted in art according to the symbolism suggested by St. Ambrose. According to the visions of Ezekiel (1:10) and John (Revelation 4:7), Matthew is represented by a **man** (because he begins his Gospel with Christ's genealogy), Mark is represented by the **lion** (because he begins his Gospel with the Baptist's message proclaimed in the wilderness), Luke is represented by the **ox** (because the sacrifice offered by Zechariah is recorded in the opening verses of his Gospel) and John is represented by the **eagle** (because of the sublime heights reached in his prologue).

**Eve.** The wife of Adam and mother of all the living. She yielded to the temptation of Satan and Adam followed her example, thus disobeying God and losing all the great spiritual gifts He had bestowed on them. However, God promised that a Redeemer would come to atone for their sin.

**Faithful.** A person with heart and mind firmly fixed on God and intent on carrying out His will on earth.

**Fear of God.** Means "holy awe," rather than real fear, in the presence of God or His messengers; the reaction of a poor sinner when confronted with infinite Goodness.

**Figure.** A person, event or object, which in God's intention, signifies or foreshadows something else. Many realities of the Old Testament foreshadowed those of the New.

**Fire.** When used metaphorically, fire means. (1) **In man**—burning zeal or ardent passion. (2) **In God**—His glory and majesty, His gift of grace to illumine and strengthen. May also denote purification and the exclusive love of God.

**Firstborn.** In the Old Testament God decreed that each firstborn male child (and each firstborn animal) be consecrated to Him. Jesus, the Firstborn of all creation, summed up in Himself the firstfruits of all creatures.

**Flesh and Blood.** (1) Synonym for man in contrast to God or pure spirits. Also used for (2) mortal man in a fallen state and (3) man as a natural rather than supernatural being.

**Frankincense.** A fragrant gum bought by the Hebrews from traders and burned at their altars, which gave sweet-smelling smoke.

**Gabriel.** The Angel who was given the honor of asking Mary to become the Mother of God. He also appeared to Zechariah to announce the birth of John the Baptist.

**Gentiles.** A word derived from the Latin meaning "foreigners." The Israelites referred to all other peoples as Gentiles.

**Glory.** Manifestation of God's presence under various forms. Also refers to **heavenly** glory. **Render glory to God** signifies acknowledgment and thanksgiving for God's power.

**Gospel.** The good news of salvation brought to the world by Jesus Christ and recorded in the New Testament.

**Grace.** A supernatural gift, freely bestowed by God, that lifts the soul to the supernatural sphere, making it pleasing to God and rendering every action performed under the influence of grace worthy of God's acceptance.

**Heart.** Signifies the source or center of activity in the corporal, spiritual or moral life.

**Heaven (Heavens).** Refers to: (1) part of the visible world (the sky); (2) the dwelling place of God, the Angels and Saints; (3) God Himself at times, e.g., Kingdom of Heaven (Kingdom of God).

**Hell.** Used by the Jews for the place where after death the souls of all led a shadow-like existence. For Christians it is used to mean the place and state of the eternal punishment of those rejected by God at their death. In the Apostles' Creed it refers to Limbo—where the just souls of the Old Testament waited in the state of natural happiness till heaven's doors were reopened by Christ.

**Herod.** Herod "the Great" was appointed by Rome as king of Judea in 40 B.C. He slaughtered the infants at Bethlehem.

**Holocaust.** A sacrifice in which the victim was entirely consumed by fire. Also used for the complete offering of self.

**Hosanna.** An exclamation of joy which means "save me." It was used by the people when Jesus entered Jerusalem in triumph as an exclamation of praise.

**Isaac.** Son of Abraham, whose sacrifice God ordered, then prevented, prefigures the sacrifice of Christ.

**Isaiah.** One of the four Major Prophets who lived in Jerusalem in the 8th century B.C. and prophesied especially concerning the Passion of our Lord.

**Israel.** Name given by God to Jacob. Also used for his descendants and for the Church (the New Israel).

**Jacob.** Son of Isaac and Rebekah and twin brother of Esau, whose birthright he took. Renamed Israel by God.

**Jeremiah.** One of the Major Prophets who prefigures the Messiah mainly by his personal sufferings.

**Jerusalem.** Capital of Israel, founded by David (also called City of David). The Church is the New Jerusalem and the image of the Heavenly Jerusalem (Heaven).

**Jesse.** The father of David and an ancestor of Jesus.

**Jonah.** One of the 12 Minor Prophets.

**Joseph.** Son of Jacob, regarded by the Liturgy as a figure of the just man and the spouse of Mary. Also refers to the tribe of Israel, subdivided into Ephraim and Manasseh.

**Judah.** Son of Jacob and ancestor of the tribe of Israel whose capital was Jerusalem. After the schism of the 10 northern tribes, it became the kingdom of Judah or Judea.

**Justice of God.** The real intrinsic holiness and justice that God imparts to a man, transforming him from a sinner into a son of God by adoption, and an heir of heaven.

**Kingdom of God or Kingdom of Heaven.** In the Old Testament the Kingdom of God represents: (1) the universal rule of God over all creatures; (2) the Hebrew nation; (3) the Messianic Kingdom that would be instituted by the Messiah. In the New Testament, this Kingdom is described as having been established by Jesus and pertains to the present and **future** (it will be consummated in heaven).

**Lamb of God.** Jesus is called the "Lamb" and "Lamb of God" to show that He bears the sins of all and offers Himself as a sacrificial lamb. The paschal lamb through whose blood the Israelites were saved from their Egyptian bondage was a figure of the true Lamb of God through Whose Blood all people were freed from the slavery of sin.

**Law.** The Law (primarily the Ten Commandments) God gave to the Chosen People was concerned mostly with external obedience. The New Law was instituted by Christ and is based on charity (which sums up the Ten Commandments). It requires both internal and external obedience.

**Levites.** Members of the tribe of Levi, who assisted the priests in Temple worship. In the parable of the Good Samaritan, the Levite failed to help his neighbor (Luke 10:32).

**Light.** Has various meanings in Scripture: (1) material sense of outward light or daybreak; (2) symbol of God (showing His incorporeal, pure and holy nature); (3) symbol of Christ; (4) Christians are children of light because they have received the spiritual light of truth and grace and are to radiate it in the world by their good example.

**Locusts.** Grasshoppers that travel in huge numbers and destroy crops.

**Lord (God) of Hosts.** Expresses God's supremacy over earthly and heavenly agencies, which He can command to His purposes (emphasizing especially His omnipotence).

**Magi.** Wise men from the East who brought gifts to Jesus in Bethlehem. Also called Astrologers.

**Man.** The Jews considered man from the viewpoint of religion—as a being dependent on God for his life. The Christian has two men within him: the "old man," drawn to evil, made up of body and soul; and the "new man" created by the Holy Spirit, who must triumph over sin.

**Manna.** Food miraculously supplied by God to the Israelites during their 40 years in the desert. Type of the Holy Eucharist—the Bread from Heaven.

**Mediator.** Christ, the God-Man, the Mediator between God and man, reconciling us to God by His death on the Cross. Each one must consent to and cooperate with the redemption freely bestowed on us by our Savior.

**Mercy.** Stems from the goodness of God that the sins of man may obscure but can never destroy. It is the free act by which God chooses someone or brings back a sinner.

**Messiah**. A Hebrew word signifying to be consecrated priest or king by an anointing.

**Moabites.** An ancient people of Palestine, inhabiting a district east of the Jordan and the Dead Sea, in constant conflict with the Israelites.

**Moses.** The leader and lawgiver of the Israelites. He successfully brought them out of Egypt, through the desert, to the shores of the Jordan. On Mount Sinai he received the Law, which contained the ethical teaching.

**Myrrh.** An odorous resin.

**Mysteries.** Supernatural truths that can be known only through revelation. The "mysteries of God," those which have God for their Author, refer to the doctrines and Sacraments preached and administered by the Apostles.

**Name.** In biblical language the name is identical with the person it designates. The name of God indicates God Himself and all His perfections. "To act in the name" of someone means to participate in the reality (and its power) expressed by this name. Change of vocation also requires a new name (e.g., Jesus, Peter).

**Nehemiah.** Cupbearer of the Persian King Cyrus, who helped to reestablish the Jewish Commonwealth after the Babylonian Captivity.

**Noah.** Patriarch who, with his family, was saved in the Ark from the Flood.

**Oil.** A perfumed ointment used especially at banquets.

**Parable.** In the New Testament spiritual truths are often communicated in the form of a story (either true or fictitious). Many of these parables teach lessons about the Kingdom of God, its members and their duties.

**Paradise.** The abode of the just souls under the old dispensation, who were waiting in Limbo for the coming of the Messiah to lead them to heaven.

**Passover.** Feast instituted to commemorate the departure from Egypt with the "passing over" of the Angel of death and the crossing of the Red Sea. Each Israelite family (as their ancestors had done) sacrificed a lamb and ate it, following a minutely described rite with unleavened bread and bitter herbs. At this observance (Last Supper), Jesus instituted the Holy Eucharist.

**Peace.** In addition to its ordinary meaning of the absence of war, it also means the possession of goods, riches, good fortune and health. Form of greeting equal to "hello"

**Pentateuch.** The first five Books of the Old Testament.

**Pharisees.** Jewish sect that sought the perfect expression of spiritual life through strict observance of the Law and tradition alone.

**Philistines.** Non-Semitic invaders who gave their name to all of Palestine, although they occupied only its southwestern plains.

**Poor.** Means more than lack of material goods. It refers to the spiritual dispositions of human beings who are conscious of their precarious condition as creatures, disdainful of everything that is not God in Whom they place their confidence and love.

**Priests.** Sacred ministers, whose duty it was to offer sacrifice.

**Prophets.** Men chosen by God to speak in His name. They were the teachers and guardians of the religion of Israel, at times advisers to kings, defenders of the poor and oppressed, heralds of the future Messiah and His Kingdom.

**Rabbi.** Signifies "My Master."

**Redemption.** Deliverance procured by payment of a ransom. Refers to the deliverance of the human race from sin, its effects and punishments, by Jesus Christ, Who by shedding His Blood on the Cross paid the price of our salvation. Prefigured by the deliverance of Israel from bondage in Egypt and Babylonia. See **Captivity.**

**Right Hand (Sit at).** To hold the place of honor.

**Sadducees.** A religious party of the Jews who were the nationalists of their day. They believed in God but rejected the oral traditions of their forefathers and denied the resurrection of human beings and the existence of Angels.

**Saints.** A common term in the Old Testament to designate those who belong to God, it was applied in the New Testament to those who believed in Christ.

**Samaritans.** Inhabitants of the central region of Palestine between Judea and Galilee who were a mixed race, descendants of the intermarriage of Israelites and Assyrian colonists, and very hostile to the Jews at the time of Christ. Originally, Samaria was the capital of the Northern Kingdom of Israel from 900 to its fall in 722 B.C.

**Sandals.** Shoes strapped to the foot with leather thongs.

**Sanhedrin.** Civil and religious Council of the Jews comprised of seventy-one members and presided over by the High Priest.

**Satan.** God's great adversary who seeks to destroy people. This devil or prince of demons is a spirit completely given up to evil. Christ crushed his power through His death.

**Scribes.** Jews devoted to the study of the Law.

**Scroll.** A roll of parchment or papyrus on which it was the custom to write.

**Semites.** A group of people whose home is Asia and Africa, reputed descendants of Shem, son of Noah. It comprises four groups: Babylonian-Assyrian, Canaanite, Aramaic and Arabian. These are marked by the same language, traits and character.

**Son of Man.** A Messianic title found in the Prophet Daniel and used by Jesus, Who by means of it progressively revealed Himself as the Messiah to the Jews.

**Soul.** A spirit having understanding and free will and destined to live forever. It is created by God to His image and likeness and is the seat of grace and glory.

**Synagogue.** A place where the Jews gathered on the Sabbath to listen to the explanation of the Bible. Each locality had one in place of the Temple of Jerusalem.

**Tabernacle.** This signifies "tent" and was originally a portable construction that served as a sanctuary for the Israelites and contained the Ark of the Covenant

**Temple.** House of worship that was built by Solomon, destroyed and then rebuilt after the Babylonian Captivity, and finally destroyed in 70 A.D., by the Romans. The Body of Christ is the new temple built at His Resurrection. The Church is the spiritual temple made up of living bricks who are the baptized Christians.

**Thanksgiving.** Was recommended many times by Jesus. He gave thanks to His Father before working miracles (John 6:11), at the Last Supper (Matthew 26:27), at the tomb of Lazarus (John 11:41).

**Word of God.** (1) A decree, commandment or utterance of God; (2) divine revelation, especially that contained in the Gospel; (3) Second Person of the Blessed Trinity.

**World.** Signifies all creation; also humans in revolt against God. The spirit of the world or the Prince of the world is a power that enslaves human beings; Jesus is their Savior.

**Wrath of God.** Not a passion or similar to the effects of human anger, but humanly speaking, (1) His hatred toward sin, aversion from a sinner, vindictive justice: (2) results of this justice, the punishments inflicted by it.

**Yahweh.** The proper personal name of the God of Israel, signifying, "I am who am" (Exodus 3:14-15). It is commonly explained in reference to God as the absolute and necessary Being. It may be understood of God as the Source of all created beings.

**Zion.** Hill on which the Temple of Jerusalem was built. It may refer to the Holy City itself and the whole nation.

# ARMENIA, ASSYRIA, ETC.

© 1984 CATHOLIC PUBLISHING CO., N.Y.

SCALE IN MILES

0   100   200   300

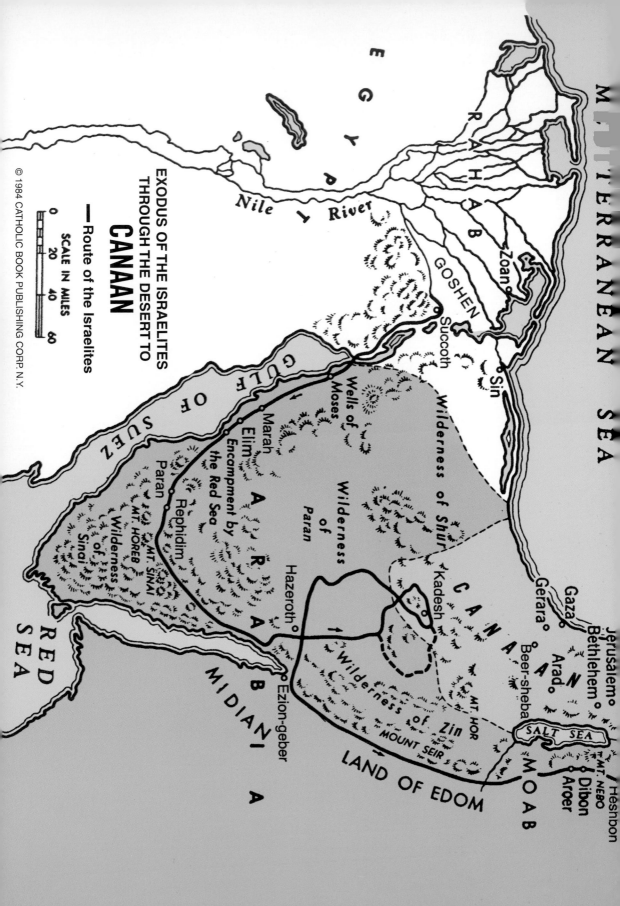

EXODUS OF THE ISRAELITES
THROUGH THE DESERT TO
**CANAAN**

— Route of the Israelites

SCALE IN MILES

0   20   40   60

© 1984 CATHOLIC BOOK PUBLISHING CORP. N.Y.

MEDITERRANEAN SEA

E G Y P T

Nile River

R A H A B

Zoan

GOSHEN

Succoth

Sin

Wilderness of Shur

Wells of Moses

Marah

Elim

Encampment by the Red Sea

GULF OF SUEZ

Paran

MT. HOREB

MT. SINAI

Rephidim

Wilderness of Sinai

A R A B

Wilderness of Paran

Hazeroth

Ezion-geber

M I D I A N

A

RED SEA

Kadesh

MT. HOR

Wilderness of Zin

MOUNT SEIR

LAND OF EDOM

C A N A A N

Gerara

Gaza

Arad

Beer-sheba

Bethlehem

Jerusalem

SALT SEA

Heshbon

MT. NEBO

Dibon

Aroer

M O A B

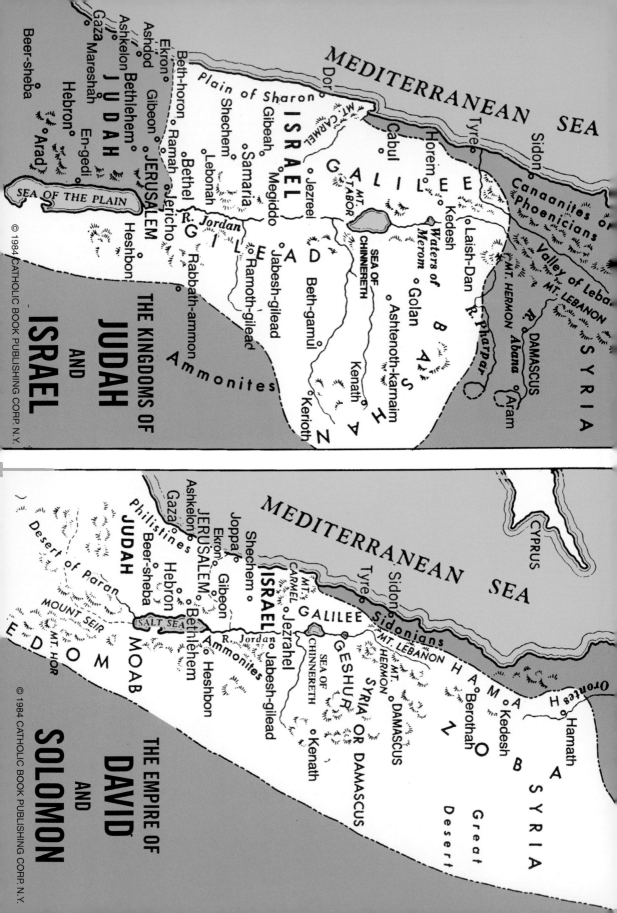

**THE KINGDOMS OF JUDAH AND ISRAEL**

MEDITERRANEAN SEA

Beer-sheba
Gaza
Ashkelon
Ashdod
Ekron
Gibeon
Beth-horon
Ramah
Bethel
Jericho
Heshbon
JERUSALEM
Bethlehem
Mareshah
Hebron
En-gedi
Arad
JUDAH

Plain of Sharon
Dor
MT. CARMEL
Shechem
Gibeah
Samaria
Lebonah
Megiddo
Jezreel
ISRAEL
GALILEE
MT. TABOR
Cabul
Horem
Tyre
Sidon
Canaanites or Phoenicians
Valley of Leba
MT. LEBANON
MT. HERMON
Abana
DAMASCUS
Aram
Kedesh
Waters of Merom
Laish-Dan
R. Pharpar
SYRIA

SEA OF THE PLAIN
R. Jordan
GILEAD
Rabbath-ammon
Jabesh-gilead
Ramoth-gilead
Beth-gamul
SEA OF CHINNERETH
Golan
Ashtenoth-karnaim
BASHAN
Kenath
Kerioth
Ammonites

© 1984 CATHOLIC BOOK PUBLISHING CORP. N.Y.

---

**THE EMPIRE OF DAVID AND SOLOMON**

MEDITERRANEAN SEA

Desert of Paran
MOUNT SEIR
MT. HOR
EDOM
Beer-sheba
Hebron
Bethlehem
Gaza
Ashkelon
Ekron
Gibeon
JERUSALEM
Joppa
Shechem
Philistines
JUDAH
SALT SEA
MOAB
R. Jordan
Heshbon
Ammonites
Jabesh-gilead

ISRAEL
MT. CARMEL
Jezrahel
GALILEE
SEA OF CHINNERETH
Kenath
GESHUR
SYRIA OR DAMASCUS
MT. HERMON
DAMASCUS
Tyre
Sidon
Sidonians
MT. LEBANON
Berothah
Kedesh
HAMATH
Great Desert
ZOBAH
SYRIA
Hamath
Orontes
CYPRUS

© 1984 CATHOLIC BOOK PUBLISHING CORP. N.Y.

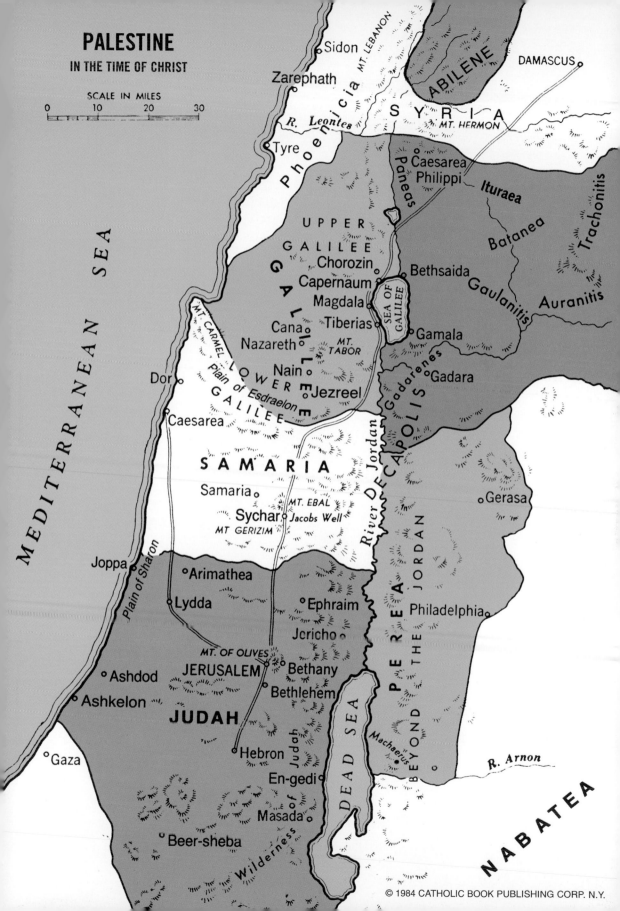

# PALESTINE
## IN THE TIME OF CHRIST

SCALE IN MILES

0    10    20    30

MEDITERRANEAN SEA

Sidon

Zarephath

ABILENE

DAMASCUS

SYRIA

MT. LEBANON

R. Leontes

Phoenicia

MT. HERMON

Tyre

Caesarea Philippi

Paneas

Ituraea

UPPER GALILEE

Chorozin

Capernaum

Bethsaida

Batanea

Trachonitis

Magdala

SEA OF GALILEE

Gaulanitis

Auranitis

Cana

Tiberias

Nazareth

MT. TABOR

Gamala

GALILEE

LOWER GALILEE

MT. CARMEL

Plain of Esdraelon

Nain

Jezreel

Gadarenes

Gadara

DECAPOLIS

Dor

River De Jordan

Caesarea

SAMARIA

Samaria

MT. EBAL

Jacobs Well

Gerasa

Sychar

MT GERIZIM

Plain of Sharon

Joppa

Arimathea

Ephraim

Philadelphia

Lydda

Jericho

River Jordan

BEYOND THE JORDAN

PEREA

MT. OF OLIVES

Bethany

JERUSALEM

Ashdod

Bethlehem

Ashkelon

JUDAH

Judah

Hebron

Wilderness

DEAD SEA

Machaerus

R. Arnon

Gaza

En-gedi

of Judah

Masada

Beer-sheba

NABATEA

© 1984 CATHOLIC BOOK PUBLISHING CORP. N.Y.

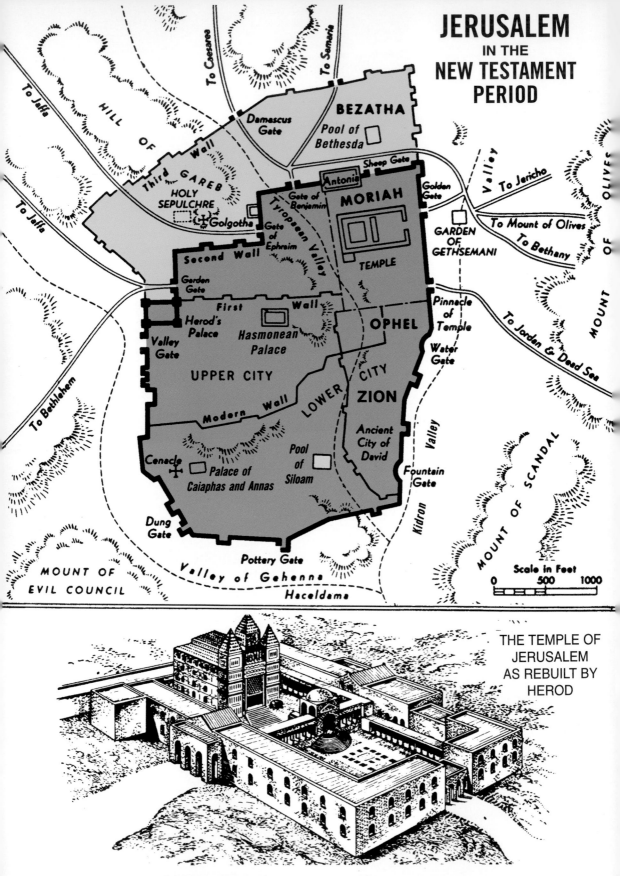

# JERUSALEM
## IN THE
## NEW TESTAMENT PERIOD

HILL OF

To Caesarea

To Samaria

To Jaffa

BEZATHA

Damascus Gate

Pool of Bethesda

Third Wall

GAREB

HOLY SEPULCHRE

Golgotha

Second Wall

To Jaffa

Garden Gate

Gate of Benjamin

Gate of Ephraim

Tyropaean Valley

Antonia

Sheep Gate

MORIAH

Golden Gate

Valley

To Jericho

GARDEN OF GETHSEMANI

To Mount of Olives

To Bethany

TEMPLE

First Wall

Herod's Palace

Hasmonean Palace

Valley Gate

UPPER CITY

Modern Wall

LOWER CITY

OPHEL

Pinnacle of Temple

Water Gate

CITY

ZION

To Jordan & Dead Sea

MOUNT OF OLIVES

Conacle

Palace of Caiaphas and Annas

Pool of Siloam

Ancient City of David

Valley

Fountain Gate

Kidron

MOUNT OF SCANDAL

Dung Gate

Pottery Gate

Valley of Gehenna

Haceldama

MOUNT OF EVIL COUNCIL

Scale in Feet

0    500    1000

THE TEMPLE OF JERUSALEM AS REBUILT BY HEROD

© 1984 CATHOLIC BOOK PUBLISHING CORP. N.Y.

# OTHER OUTSTANDING CATHOLIC BOOKS
## FOR CHILDREN

**ILLUSTRATED BOOK OF SAINTS**— By Rev. Thomas J. Donaghy. Over 80 of the most beloved and recognizable Saints are included in this new volume. Each Saint is vividly described in two full pages: one page details the life and legacy of the Saint, and the other page offers a magnificently striking full-color illustration. Certain to be a source of information and visual delight for years to come.    **Ask for No. 735.**

**MY FIRST COMMUNION**—This gloriously illustrated keepsake album is a special way to help a child remember the first time he or she receives the Eucharist. Memories of the people, prayers, reflections, photos, mementos and activities leading to and celebrating a child's First Communion Day are beautifully bound in this sturdy treasury.    **Ask for No. 830.**

**PICTURE BOOK OF PRAYERS**—New beautiful book of prayers for children featuring prayers for the day, major feasts, various occasions and special days: First Communion, Confirmation, Name Day and Birthday.
    **Ask for No. 265.**

**NEW FIRST MASS BOOK**—Ideal Children's Mass Book with all the official Mass prayers. Full-color illustrations of the Mass and the Life of Christ. Confession and Communion Prayers.    **Ask for No. 808.**

**PICTURE BOOK OF SAINTS**—By Rev. L. Lovasik, S.V.D. Illustrated lives of the Saints in full color for young and old. It clearly depicts the lives of over 100 popular Saints in word and picture.    **Ask for No. 235.**

**ILLUSTRATED LIFE OF JESUS**—By Rev. L. Lovasik, S.V.D. A large-format book with magnificent full-color pictures for young readers to enjoy and learn about the life of Jesus. With simple, easy-to-read language, this timeless book about the greatest life ever lived will be treasured by all who use it.    **Ask for No. 935.**

**MY GUARDIAN ANGEL**—By Rev.Thomas J. Donaghy. New inspiring book about Guardian Angels that will teach children about Angels and the part they play in our lives. 16 beautiful illustrations in full color.
    **Ask for No. 125.**

**THE MASS FOR CHILDREN**—By Rev. Jude Winkler, OFM Conv. Beautifully illustrated Mass Book that explains the Mass to children and contains the Mass responses they should know. It is sure to help children know and love the Mass.    **Ask for No. 215.**

## WHEREVER CATHOLIC BOOKS ARE SOLD